After the Tomb

The Unexpected Encore

Stephen Austin

scrivinspire

Copyright © 2025 by Stephen Austin

Published by ScrivInspire,
an imprint of Scrivenings Press LLC
15 Lucky Lane
Morrilton, Arkansas 72110
https://ScriveningsPress.com

Printed in the United States of America

All rights reserved. No part of this publication may be reproduced, stored in a retrieval system, or transmitted in any form or by any means—for example, electronic, photocopy and recording— without the prior written permission of the publisher. The only exception is brief quotations in printed reviews.

Paperback ISBN 978-1-64917-446-8

eBook ISBN 978-1-64917-447-5

Editors: Sally Crossley and Linda Fulkerson

Cover by Linda Fulkerson www.bookmarketinggraphics.com

Scripture quotations taken from The Holy Bible, New International Version® NIV® Copyright © 1973, 1978, 1984, 2011 by Biblica, Inc. Used with permission. All rights reserved worldwide.

Maps and Images in Appendix C are used with permission from BiblePlaces.com and *Satellite Bible Atlas*.

NO AI TRAINING: Without in any way limiting the author's [and publisher's] exclusive rights under copyright, any use of this publication to "train" generative artificial intelligence (AI) technologies to generate text is expressly prohibited. The author reserves all rights to license uses of this work for generative AI training and development of machine learning language models.

This book is dedicated to three people in particular, among others, who encouraged me through the process of writing and editing this book:

- My wife Lynette, with whom I began to talk about this book 12 years ago on a night-time walk, and who made valuable suggestions about writing and framing, as well as affirming that this book could be unique and important;
- My sister Marcia, an accomplished biblical scholar who shares my love for and interest in this kind of biblical imagination and wonder, and who spent more than 100 hours editing the manuscript;
- And my mother-in-law Wynetta, who along the way fed me her beef stew as she encouraged me in writing the book, asked about my progress, and read early drafts.

Contents

Introduction	ix
Preface	xi
Vignette 1 *The Centurion Believes*	1
Vignette 2 *Joseph of Arimathea and Pilate*	3
Vignette 3 *Caiaphas Celebrates*	7
Vignette 4 *From the Cross to the Tomb*	11
Vignette 5 *Peter's Dark Night*	15
Vignette 6 *Anguish in Bethany*	17
Vignette 7 *Nicodemus' Confession*	21
Vignette 8 *The Moment the World Changed Forever*	25
Vignette 9 *Jesus and Mary Magdalene*	29
Vignette 10 *"He Does Not Treat Us As Our Sins Deserve"*	33
Vignette 11 *The Best Torah Lesson in History*	37
Vignette 12 *Who Are These People? (Part 1)*	45
Vignette 13 *Celebration in Bethany*	49
Vignette 14 *The Intriguing Case of Lazarus*	53
Vignette 15 *An Unforgettable Walk to Bethlehem*	59
Vignette 16 *Tragedy in Bethlehem, Revisited*	63
Vignette 17 *Jesus Confronts Caiaphas*	67

Vignette 18 The "Man from the Dream" Visits Pilate and Procla	71
Vignette 19 Who are These People? (Part 2)	75
Vignette 20 Return to Golgotha	79
Vignette 21 A New Vision for Bartimaeus	87
Vignette 22 A Fresh Start for Zacchaeus	93
Vignette 23 A Changed Woman, a Changed Village	97
Vignette 24 The Grateful Leper	103
Vignette 25 Two Trips to Heaven, Two Resurrections	107
Vignette 26 Confessions at Breakfast	115
Vignette 27 Day of Testimony	121
Vignette 28 Supper at Matthew's House	127
Vignette 29 A New Celebration	133
Vignette 30 A Sober Delivery from Joseph of Arimathea	137
Vignette 31 Taming the Sons of Thunder	141
Vignette 32 Life in Cana After the Wedding	147
Vignette 33 Reckoning Time for Antipas	153
Vignette 34 A Second Chance to Follow	159
Vignette 35 The Delivered Decapolis Demoniac	167
Vignette 36 The Circle Closes—Coming Near to God Again	173
Vignette 37 Lunch with the Rabbi of Nazareth	181
Vignette 38 Storytime Under the Olive Tree	187

Vignette 39 Would You Like to Write a Gospel?	193
Vignette 40 Get out of the Boat!	199
Vignette 41 A Special Wedding in Caesarea Philippi	205
Vignette 42 More than Five Hundred—the Galilean Believers	211
Vignette 43 I Give You My Mind and My Spirit	217
Vignette 44 You Will Drink the Cup I Drink	221
Vignette 45 The Testimony of the Risen Saints	227
Vignette 46 We Were Blind, But Now We See	237
Vignette 47 He Stopped Sinning, and Something Better Happened to Him	243
Vignette 48 New Life After Being Rescued	249
Vignette 49 Final Words, Final Miracle	253
Vignette 50 Pentecost in the Temple—the Church is Born	257
Appendix A: Notes, Scriptures & References	267
Appendix B: Resources Consulted	289
Appendix C: Maps & Images	299
Acknowledgments	313
About the Author	315
You May Also Like:	317

Introduction
Author's Note

As a Christian, Bible professor, and minister, I've studied and taught about the life of Christ for more than forty years. About twelve years ago, while reading the stories of Jesus' appearances after his resurrection, I began to wonder what had happened during those forty days on earth before his ascension. We have biblical stories from perhaps five of those days.

Where did he go? What did he do? Who did he talk to? What topics did he discuss? The Bible has remarkably little to say about these things. And besides lessons on the few stories we do have, I have never heard any sermons or classes, read any books, nor seen any videos about this part of his ministry.

I once read a scholar's explanation of Mark's account of Jesus praying in the Garden of Gethsemane. He said that since no one was with Jesus when he prayed (apart from sleeping disciples), that Mark must have just invented that part of the story.

What an unfortunate conclusion! Rather, I think it is much more likely that Jesus spoke in detail with his disciples about the events of his arrest and trial during the forty days he was with them. If I were

Introduction

an apostle, that would have been one of the first questions I asked after his resurrection.

I believe during these forty days, Jesus planted the seeds for many things that happened later, such as the beginning of the church, the gospels, and the apostles' ministries. Acts 1:3 says Jesus spoke with them during this time about the Kingdom of God; all these topics would be part of his Kingdom.

I believe he talked with his mother and family, visited people whom he had healed or helped, and taught and encouraged them regarding their roles in the kingdom.

I believe this was a time of joy and celebration after the suffering and sorrow of his trial and death.

In this book, I've begun with the biblical account, then added my description of what Jesus might have done or said during the forty days. I used "biblical imagination," often basing my ideas on scriptural principles or events shown in other parts of Jesus' ministry. I've included many references to scriptural events and principles that informed my thinking and writing, as well as consulting many other historical and cultural sources.

I don't claim that the events I write about happened—but I think they are possible, even likely.

I pray this book will help its readers ponder deeply the character and ministry of Jesus and how they can follow in his footsteps.

Stephen Austin
sraustin7724@gmail.com

Preface
The Third Omer

When the Israelites traveled from Egypt to Mount Sinai to receive the Law, the Lord began to provide food for them in the desert, which he continued until three days after they reached the Promised Land. The Israelites gathered their *omer* of manna each day to sustain them physically in the desert. God also gave them a second kind of *omer*—a wordplay spelled a little differently in Hebrew but sounding the same. This *omer* was God's Law—his promises, commands, and words—which sustained them spiritually through the desert. Jesus is the first and the second *omer*—the Bread of Life, the Word of God, the Promise of God. Through these things, he can sustain us forever.

The Jews also celebrate a third *omer*—the 50 days between Passover and Pentecost. In Exodus, this was the time when the Israelites waited to receive the laws and promises of God at Mount Sinai. Over the years, it has become a time of waiting for the Messiah, which some Jews think will happen on Pentecost. The year Jesus died, this *omer* began on Resurrection Sunday and ended on Pentecost Sunday with the establishment of the church.

This book tracks what Jesus might have done during the third *omer,* preparing for the full coming of the Spirit and establishment of

Preface

the church. I present 50 vignettes, one for each day of the *omer*, offering a chronological path and itinerary Jesus *might* have taken. I invite you to come on this journey to reflect with me what those days could have been like, learn more about Jesus and Israel, and consider what purposes he has for you and me as we wait for his return.

Stephen Austin

Vignette 1

The Centurion Believes

John 19:17-37; Matthew 27:51-55

"It is finished," Jesus cried, and his head fell forward on his chest. The small group of women near the foot of Jesus' cross wailed.

The centurion glanced up at the man, then felt the earth begin to shake under his feet. Large rocks in the quarry nearby split open and crashed to the ground.

The two criminals screamed as the tremors rattled their crosses.

The Roman soldiers stationed near the cross grabbed their swords, looking ready to fight or run.

The spectators ran away shrieking, scrambling for safety.

A series of loud cracks erupted from several tombs in the garden near the crosses. Many stones, which had covered the mouths of graves, toppled over. Jagged lines opened along the face of rocks. Through the gloom, the centurion caught a glimpse of movement. Shrouded figures emerged from the tombs and came toward the crosses.

Choking down a scream of terror, the centurion broke and ran, his men racing behind him down the path toward the nearby city wall. They charged through the Gennath gate, fled headlong through the streets, and finally reached the gate of the Antonia Fortress, where they leaned against the walls, panting. The centurion gazed toward Golgotha, slowly regaining his wits and calming his racing heart, drew a shuddering breath, and declared, "Surely ... that man was the Son of God!"

Reflect

1. Why do you think there was such a variety of responses from the people present at the cross that day?
2. If you are a follower of Jesus, what convinced you he was the Son of God? If you are not, what do you think *would* convince you?

Learn

In order to understand the gospels better, study a good map of Jerusalem during the time of Jesus. (See maps of Jerusalem in Appendix C.)

Vignette 2

Joseph of Arimathea and Pilate

John 18:33-38; Matthew 27:57-61

"It is finished." Still shaken from the last anguished cry of Jesus on the cross, still fearful because of the terrifying earthquake and darkness, Joseph of Arimathea hurried after the centurion, toward the Antonia Fortress, hoping his wealth and position on the Sanhedrin would gain him an audience with Pilate.

At the fortress gate, Joseph asked the guards if he could speak with Pilate. After hesitating briefly, they led him to Pilate's chambers. Shrieks of terror from the street penetrated the walls and mixed with shouts of confusion inside the fortress courtyard.

Turning abruptly toward Joseph, Pilate barked, "What do you want?"

"Procurator, as you probably know, the man Jesus has died," Joseph responded. "With your permission, I'd like to take his body and give it a proper burial."

"He's dead already? The criminals usually last for days."

"Yes—but I saw him die. The soldiers confirmed it by piercing his side with a spear."

Glancing over at the centurion, who had followed Joseph into the chamber, Pilate asked, "Is this true?"

"Yes, Procurator. We also saw him perish," he confirmed.

Pilate paused a moment, then queried Joseph, "But why do *you* want the body?"

Joseph hoped Pilate didn't know he was a secret disciple of Jesus. "Sir, he is a sincere teacher of the law, as well as a good man. As you yourself said earlier today, it doesn't seem he committed a crime worthy of death. May I be of service to you by taking care of his body?"

Pilate assented with a curt nod, and Joseph departed hastily from the room, relieved.

Of all the irritating, confusing, and troublesome situations Pilate had faced with the Jews, this was the worst. Joseph was right—Pilate was still not convinced of the Nazarene's guilt. How had he let himself be trapped by the power-hungry high priest, Caiaphas, and his accomplices? True, it was good to avoid a riot, which might have caused trouble for him in Rome and damaged his career. But he couldn't evade the memory of the prisoner's supernaturally calm face as he asserted, "My kingdom is from another place … everyone who is on the side of truth listens to me … You would have no power over me if it were not given to you from above."

Even at that late stage, Pilate had been sure that given the choice to free a prisoner, the Jews would ask him for Jesus, if he were really their king, rather than the murderer Barabbas. Instead, the same people who insisted on their one sovereign God astonished him with the brazen lie, "We have no king but Caesar!"

Pilate was trapped. If the crowd recognized the authority of Caesar, the representative of Caesar could not go against them. The decision had been neatly snatched from his hands. So, he turned and washed them of the sorry affair.

Reflect

1. How did Jesus challenge Pilate's perception of power and control?
2. Pilate ignored Jesus' words and clear evidence of innocence in order to avoid political problems. What would cause you to ignore and disobey Jesus?

Learn

See how the geographical background of the gospels can impact your understanding of the stories. Bargil Pixner wrote a fascinating, well-illustrated book about Jesus' ministry in Jerusalem: Pixner, Bargil. *With Jesus in Jerusalem: His First and Last Days in Judea*. Rosh Pina: Corazin Publishing, 2005.

Vignette 3
Caiaphas Celebrates

Matthew 26:57-68; Luke 22:50-51; John 7:45-49; 8:59

"It is finished! Finally!" exulted Caiaphas. Back at his home in southwest Jerusalem, he had just received the news of Jesus' quick death. "After three years of constant trouble from the Galilean, we are rid of him."

His servant Malchus, who had been strangely silent all day, murmured, "Yes, we are."

Caiaphas continued, "So many times we were close, but he would disappear in the Temple crowds. He even seemed to convince some of the Temple guards, or the priests—and Joseph of Arimathea was reluctant to speak against him last night."

Malchus rubbed his ear. "He was an unusual man. It's almost as if he thought he really were the Messiah …"

"And that was his downfall!" declared Caiaphas. "If I hadn't trapped him into admitting who he was, we might have had to set him free. But fools like him always delude themselves. He had the audacity to say he was the Messiah, that he fulfilled Daniel's prophecy of being the Son of Man. After that, it was easy for the

Council to declare blasphemy and sentence him. Then, when we maneuvered Pilate into a corner, he had to send him to the cross."

Caiaphas smiled smugly, savoring his victory. "One of my finest moments as High Priest—one man died instead of our whole nation perishing."

Silence ensued instead of the fawning approval Caiaphas expected. He glanced over at Malchus. "What's wrong with you? Why do you keep touching your ear?"

"It's just that—last night, something strange happened," Malchus ventured.

"Everything was strange last night," blustered Caiaphas, impatiently. "What are you talking about?"

"When you sent me to the garden of Gethsemane with the soldiers to arrest him," Malchus said, "first Judas identified the rabbi. Jesus didn't even try to deny who he was or escape. Rather, he asked who we sought. When the soldiers said they were seeking him, he simply told us to let his disciples go."

"So? He probably realized his charade was about to end."

"Well, right then, one of his disciples lunged at me and swung his sword. I tried to duck, but the edge of the sword sliced through my ear, and a wave of pain rushed through my head. Blood gushed down my face and neck. I staggered and fell, and my ear was lying on the ground beside me. It was a nightmare!"

Caiaphas scoffed, "But Malchus, that's ridiculous. I can see your ears, and they are fine. You must not remember what happened."

"No," contradicted Malchus, looking quickly at Caiaphas, "I remember it—I just can't quite believe it. As I groped around on the ground to find my ear, Jesus told his disciple to put away his sword. Then, Jesus knelt beside me and gently placed his hand over the wound.

"For a moment, it was as if he and I were the only ones there. The sounds of the others died away. His eyes radiated compassion and concern for me, even while the soldiers were arresting him. My pain and panic were slowly replaced by a peace I couldn't understand. Jesus gave me a slight smile and stood.

"When I touched the spot where the sword had sliced my head, I realized I wasn't bleeding. There was no wound anymore. Jesus had healed me!"

"Don't lie to me, Malchus!" Caiaphas roared. "Have you become his follower too? Get out of my sight!"

Reflect

1. Can you think of other points during Jesus´ ministry when he could have veered away from God's purposes but chose to obey?
2. What is the most useful motivation you use to remind yourself to obey when it would be easier or safer to disobey?

Learn

For more information about the illegalities of Jesus' trial with Caiaphas, see Jim Bishop's book, *The Day Christ Died*, Harper and Brothers: 1957, pp. 219-224.

VIGNETTE 4

FROM THE CROSS TO THE TOMB

Mark 15:42-47; Psalm 116:3, 7, 15; John 19:25-42

An eerie darkness still blanketed the city as Joseph left the fortress and pushed his way through the people thronging the streets. When he arrived at Golgotha, he found the faithful women and John huddled, weeping, at the foot of the cross.

The three men wrestled the cross out of the ground and laid it down. They worked the nails loose, and Joseph put them in his bag. Then, the women took the myrrh and aloes that Nicodemus had brought, rubbed them on Jesus' mangled body, and wrapped it in a linen burial cloth. The silence was profound, broken only by occasional sobs from the group as tears streamed down their faces.

Joseph, John, and Nicodemus carried the body between them, soon arriving at Joseph's new tomb, nearby. Stooping to enter, they placed the body on a shelf to one side, and the group stood gazing at the still form.

Nicodemus broke the silence, reciting part of a Passover psalm, "The snares of death encompassed me; the pangs of Sheol laid hold on me. I suffered distress and anguish. Return, O my soul, to your rest. Precious in the sight of the Lord is the death of his faithful ones."

They bowed their heads for a long moment, and then Nicodemus and Joseph moved outside and prepared to close the tomb. Shoulders shaking, Mary stepped toward her son and laid her hand on Jesus' head. John placed his arm around her, and she leaned into him. She took a deep breath and turned toward the door. The group filed from the tomb, and Joseph and Nicodemus rolled the stone over the opening.

John guided Mary as they stumbled through the darkness on their way back to Bethany, Mary leaning heavily on his arm.

Had it only been a day since they had gathered around the Passover table? What began as a normal Seder meal had suddenly changed. First, the troubling accusation that one of them would betray Jesus, then Jesus' earnest words about a new commandment and covenant, then Jesus telling Peter he would deny Jesus before the rooster crowed three times.

John had seen it with his own eyes. Peter, the brash leader, the one with the quick answer, the first out of the boat, ready to lay down his life for Jesus—this Peter had turned into a coward! Standing near the fire in Caiaphas' courtyard, John watched the servants and officials question Peter about his relationship with Jesus. Peter blustered and swore. Then, the rooster's call startled him into silence. A horrified look came over his face, and he slunk away from the door into the darkness. John had not seen him since.

The Sanhedrin delivered the verdict of guilty, sealing Jesus' fate and sending him hurtling toward the cross. John followed Jesus from Caiaphas' house to the Antonia Fortress, where he waited outside in the dark. Then came the quick trip to the western city and Herod's

After the Tomb

fortress, where the soldiers mocked Jesus with blows and dragged him back to the fortress.

John shuddered as he remembered the cruel call of the crowd, their faces twisted in anger. Some of the same people had celebrated with the disciples coming from the Mount of Olives into Jerusalem just five days earlier. How could they so easily change from "Hosanna, Son of David" to "Crucify him"?

Then came the bloodthirsty, victorious roar of the crowd, the savagely gleeful faces of the Jewish leaders, the awful slash of the whip as it chewed through the flesh on Jesus' body.

It was at that moment that Mary had collapsed onto John. He almost had to carry her through the streets, following her son Jesus to Golgotha. She buried her face in his cloak as the hammers rang out, mixed with Jesus' cries and groans. During the long hours that followed, John begged her to look away, to leave, but she refused.

Toward the end, Jesus seemed to wake from the fog of pain. He gazed down at Mary and John, and gasped out to his mother, "Woman, here is your son." Mary nodded, silent tears pouring down her face. "John, here is your mother." John pulled her to him, and she laid her head on his chest and sobbed. A new bond had formed, which would never be broken.

Now to Bethany—but then what? Where to go? What should they do? Full of doubt and sorrow, John and Mary reeled down the path.

Reflect

1. What qualities helped John be the only apostle to stay close to Jesus throughout his arrest, trial, and crucifixion?

2. What are the most important responsibilities Jesus might have given you because you follow him?

LEARN

Psalm 116 is one of the *Hallal* psalms (Psalms 113-118) used during Passover week. Read this and consider how it might have fit Jesus' crucifixion, and possibly been the song Jesus and the disciples sang at the end of the Last Supper.

Vignette 5

Peter's Dark Night

Luke 22:31-34, 54-62

Since the strange darkness at noon, Peter had stayed close to the house where the disciples had shared the last supper the night before. During the last twelve hours, that terrible conversation in Caiaphas' courtyard with the soldier and the servant girls had been seared into his heart.

Their questions stabbed him accusingly: "You also were with that Nazarene!"

"No, I was not!"

"You're one of his disciples, too, aren't you?"

"I am not!"

"Didn't I see you with him in the garden?"

"I don't know this man you're talking about!"

Jesus' words pounded in Peter's brain, "Before the rooster crows, you will deny me three times."

Then came the slow turn of Jesus' head, the gaze that fastened on Peter's face. Peter could barely look at him—was that disappointment he saw in Jesus' eyes? Anger? Sadness? Surely not … compassion?

Peter's eyes burned, and fresh tears coursed down his cheeks. He despised himself for his rash promise and for the weakness that made him crumble just hours later.

His voice broke, "Dear God! How can I face John and James? How can I ever bear to look at Mary again?"

The memory hounded him. "Simon, Simon. Satan has asked to sift you as wheat …"

Maybe it would be better to leave Jerusalem now in this darkness, to sneak back to Galilee. They would all despise him now. No one would consider following a coward.

But he clung stubbornly to Jesus' words of hope, however improbable: "I have prayed for you, that your faith may not fail, and when you have turned back, strengthen your brothers."

He didn't flee.

Yet he was miserable, desolate, and devastated.

Reflect

1. How might a Jew understand Jesus' words, "Satan has asked to sift Peter as wheat"?
2. Considering your answers, in what ways may Satan be trying to sift you?

Learn

How might Amos 9:9 help you understand this phrase? Or Nehemiah 5:13, Job 38:13, or Haggai 2:6?

Vignette 6

Anguish in Bethany

Luke 9:52-56

Martha opened the door as John and Mary arrived late Friday afternoon. Wordlessly, she and Mary fell into each other's arms. Martha took the exhausted mother to her room, helped her lie down, and went to the kitchen. By the time she returned several minutes later with a basin of warm water and a cloth, Mary's eyes had closed. Martha prayed that sleep would at least bring some measure of physical healing.

Martha sat beside the bed and gently washed Mary's face, then laid her palm on Mary's cheek for a moment, eyes brimming as she studied Mary's countenance. She took up Mary's hands, washing off the bloodstains, then bathed Mary's feet. She pondered the bloody cloth in her hands and murmured, "I can't imagine. Oh, God, give her strength! What will she do now?"

Lazarus embraced John and brought him into the living room. Exhausted, they sank onto a low couch and stared at the floor. Lazarus asked quietly, "What it was like out there today?"

John sighed. "It was terrible. He had told us he would suffer, but none of us thought it would be so cruel, so unjust.

"I remember when James and I wanted to call down fire from heaven on a Samaritan village because they rejected us, but Jesus rebuked us. Surely *today* would have been the moment for God's fire to consume these men as they crucified him. They deserved it. And yet ... from the cross, Jesus forgave them. He *forgave* them!

"I think Jesus was praying a psalm. He cried out, 'My God! My God, why have you forsaken me?' Lazarus—that psalm talks about villains dividing clothes and casting lots for garments. And the worst part of it, the psalmist says, 'He has not despised or scorned the suffering of his afflicted one; he has not hidden his face from him but has listened to his cry for help.'"

John drew a ragged breath, and a tear rolled down his cheek. "But God didn't listen to his own son today. He hid his face, and Jesus died. And now our hope is gone."

Reflect

1. On Friday and Saturday, what do you think Mary did and thought? Do you think she believed Jesus would be resurrected? What did she see in her future?
2. What impossible thing might God be ready to do for you if you are trapped in a hopeless situation?

Learn

Three times in the Hebrew text of Psalm 22 (the Masoretic text of vv. 13, 17, 22), lions threaten and attack God's righteous one, who originally was King David. Christians connect this to Jesus' experience on the cross—the death of the Lion of Judah. God rescues both David and Jesus, though in Jesus' case, it is after death, through the resurrection.

Vignette 7
Nicodemus' Confession

Deuteronomy 6:4-9

Gamaliel sat with his friend Nicodemus at Sabbath supper, prayer shawls drawn over bowed heads, candles glowing. Gamaliel recited the Sabbath Shema and the traditional blessing of the wine and bread, "Hear, O Israel, the Lord our God, the Lord is one. Blessed be His glorious name, whose kingdom is forever.

"Praise to You, Adonai, our God, Sovereign of the Universe, Creator of the fruit of the vine. Blessed are you, Adonai, our God, King of the Universe, who has brought forth bread from the earth."

As his wife served a simple Sabbath meal, Gamaliel studied his friend Nicodemus. "It has been an earth-shattering day," he ventured. "We knew it might end this way. You saw how Caiaphas became obsessed with getting rid of Jesus. He believes the traitor Judas was a godsend."

Nicodemus responded, "But we are complicit in this matter, Gamaliel. Even though Jesus was arrested, he should never have been convicted, much less killed. It was shameful how Caiaphas manipulated the Council. If only Jesus had kept silent, he might have been freed. But now we, too, are partly guilty."

"We only did what seemed necessary, as leaders," argued Gamaliel, "What if this Galilean was not the Messiah? Perhaps we have preserved our religion and protected our nation."

Nicodemus sat silent, toying with his glass.

Gamaliel probed, "Nicodemus? Is there something else?"

Nicodemus straightened up, as if shrugging off a heavy burden. He took a deep breath and met Gamaliel's eyes squarely. "I have been a secret follower of Jesus for almost three years. His teaching, his miracles, his character all convinced me. But during the last few hours, I helped sentence, crucify, and bury the true Messiah." He dropped his gaze to the table, and his lips trembled. "What kind of follower betrays his rabbi?"

Reflect

1. How might Jesus' relationship with Nicodemus, Joseph of Arimathea, and Gamaliel have impacted the early church? Could Gamaliel's warning against punishing Peter and John (Acts 5:35ff) have been influenced by his relationship with Joseph and Nicodemus? Could their relationship have influenced Gamaliel's instruction of the apostle Paul in the following years? Did any of these three possibly suffer or die for Jesus later as his followers?
2. If you are a Christian, has your relationship with Jesus put you in danger in any way? How would you handle that?

Learn

Gamaliel, Nicodemus, and Joseph of Arimathea were all members of the Sanhedrin. See this article in Britannica for further information of this group's history and duties. https://www.britannica.com/topic/Judaism/Biblical-Judaism-20th-4th-century-bce

Vignette 8
The Moment the World Changed Forever

Matthew 28:1-7

After a second wasted night guarding the tomb, Reuben was eager to head back to his quarters in Jerusalem. He stood and stretched in the fresh morning air. As the eastern sky began to brighten, Gad arrived from the city to relieve him.

"Looks like another boring day ahead," observed Gad. "How long will we have to guard a dead man?"

"Probably at least three or four days," responded Reuben. "Then maybe Caiaphas will forget about the threat from the Galilean, and we'll have no more riots—"

A violent earthquake threw both men to the ground, away from the tomb. Amid the rumbling, a bright flash like lightning came from the tomb. Lifting his head from the ground, Reuben squinted and saw what looked like a man in a white robe appear beside the stone and roll it away.

Reuben shut his eyes in disbelief, then hesitantly opened them again. Now the man sat on top of the stone. A cool wind rushed out from the tomb, raising goosebumps all over Reuben's body. It felt as though the breeze carried something intangible with it.

His entire body trembled as he struggled to comprehend what was happening. Gad's face was buried in the ground, arms over his head to protect himself from the unknown threat. Gradually, the ground stopped shaking, but Gad and Reuben remained prostrate, and the man in white stayed on the stone, eyes toward the city as if waiting for someone.

Mary Magdalene, Mary the mother of James, Joanna, and Salome moved slowly along the trail from Bethany to Golgotha. The events of Friday and the desolation of the Sabbath lay heavy on them still. They conversed in hushed voices.

"I heard that Caiaphas asked Pilate to seal the tomb and place a guard there," said Joanna. "I wonder if they'll let us anoint the body?"

"Who can help us roll away the stone? I doubt Caiaphas' soldiers will do it."

They rounded the last bend of the trail and stopped abruptly. The tomb stood open, and the stone was already rolled away. Even from a distance, they saw the burial garments lying on the shelf where Jesus had been, and the cloth that had been wrapped around Jesus' head—but no body. The linens were folded as if no longer needed.

Mary Magdalene was the last one up the trail. When she saw the empty tomb, she gasped and froze where she stood. Then she turned around and ran back toward Jerusalem, to the house where Peter and John were staying.

At almost the same instant, the other women caught sight of the angel on the stone and fell to their knees. The angel said, "Do not be afraid, for I know that you are looking for Jesus, who was crucified.

"He is not here; he has risen, just as he said. So why do you look for the living among the dead? Remember how he told you, while he was still with you in Galilee, 'The Son of Man must be delivered into the hands of sinners, be crucified, and on the third day be raised again.'"

The angel's words calmed the women. Joanna felt a glimmer of unbelievable hope. Could this possibly be true? She remembered now that Jesus had said it, but for some reason, none of them had understood what he meant.

"Come and see the place where they laid him. Then go tell his disciples, and Peter, that Jesus is going ahead of you into Galilee. You will see him there again, just as he told you!"

Ecstatic with joy, Joanna turned and hurried away from the tomb, the other women close behind.

Once more alone at the tomb, Reuben and Gad finally clambered to their feet and fled.

Reflect

1. Even though Jesus had foretold his resurrection several times (Matt. 16:21, 17:9, 23, 20:19), why did people not expect it?
2. How might you have responded differently than those in this story?

Learn

The gospel accounts of the events of Resurrection Sunday vary in some details. This article, with its graphics, is helpful in synthesizing those events. https://answersingenesis.org/jesus/resurrection/christs-resurrection-four-accounts-one-reality/

VIGNETTE 9

JESUS AND MARY MAGDALENE

Mark 16:9; Luke 8:2; John 20:11-18

On her very first encounter with Jesus, Mary Magdalene had been sitting outside her house on the outskirts of Magdala. When Jesus walked into the village, the hated demons in her head blustered, frantically, "You're in danger, Mary. Run away from that man. He wants to destroy you!"

Jolted to her feet, Mary backed up against the wall. The rabbi Jesus was almost at her house. He didn't seem dangerous, yet the voices screamed even louder. Her heart raced, and she edged toward the door, ready to hide.

But then a quiet, soothing voice said, "Mary, Mary." Suddenly, the demons' voices faded as a strange sensation began to seep into her soul. As if in a dream, she slowly raised her eyes to Jesus, who was smiling kindly at her. "Shalom, Mary. The Peace of God be with you."

Then, his voice taking on a sharp edge, Jesus declared, "Spirits! I command you to come out of her, and never trouble her again!"

The spirits that had tormented her for years stabbed her with a final flash of rage and departed forever. A blessed tranquility filled her mind and soul, bringing healing and rest. She was free!

She stepped hesitantly toward him. He held out his arms and gently embraced her. "You're my Father's daughter, Mary. You're welcome to follow me if you choose." She buried her face in his chest and sobbed.

Mary now leaned against the wall outside the tomb, the memory bringing fresh tears to her eyes. A rustling sound came from the tomb, and she looked in and saw two angels in white.

They asked her, "Woman, why are you crying?"

"They've taken my Lord away, and I don't know where they have put him," she replied and turned away, only to encounter another man standing there. She couldn't make out his face because of the dim light and the tears in her eyes.

The man asked, "Woman, why are you crying?" He glanced at the angels behind Mary and smiled at them.

"Sir, if you have carried him away, tell me where you have put him, and I will get him."

Jesus himself said to her, "Mary."

That *voice*! The one from that first day, the one she had trusted for three years as she followed him everywhere. But ...wasn't he ...

Eyes widening, mouth opening soundlessly, heart leaping, Mary faced the man. Impossibly, Jesus stood there with that same smile filled with kindness and even a spark of humor. "Teacher!" she exclaimed, and clutched his robe, her eyes searching his face.

He took her hands in his, still beaming at her. "Go to my brothers and tell them, 'I am ascending to my Father and your Father, to my God and your God.'"

He laid a warm hand on her shoulder. With one more long disbelieving look, she turned and ran happily toward the city.

Reflect

1. Why do you think several people did not recognize Jesus at first after his resurrection? (John 20:15; Mark 16:12; Luke 24:16)
2. At the beginning of her relationship with Jesus, Mary Magdalene was healed. If you are a Christian, what do you remember from the early part of your relationship with Jesus? In what ways did he change your life?

Learn

Novels and movies notwithstanding, there is no evidence Mary Magdalene had any relationship with Jesus other than as a grateful, dedicated disciple. Eastern tradition claims she went with John the Apostle to Ephesus and died there. Others think she may have evangelized part of Gaul (today's France). But none of this has been proven.

Vignette 10
"He Does Not Treat Us As Our Sins Deserve"

2 Chronicles 33:6; Acts 1:15-19; Psalm 103:8-12

After the women had left the house, Peter paced, trying to make sense of their news. Finally, the house was too small to contain him, and he wound his way through the neighborhood and out the Essene Gate set in the southwest wall of the city.

The Hinnom Valley stretched out below him. As a Jew, Peter remembered stories about how Manasseh and other evil kings came here to light fires to such gods as Molech or Baal, then sacrifice their sons to the gods. It was often a place of horror and death.

Peter descended into the valley and walked along the base of its steep southern walls. Ahead he saw vultures gathered around what was likely a dead animal of some kind. Yet as he drew near, he realized it was a dead human body. And with growing horror, he recognized part of the robe. Judas!

Peter sank to his knees and shut his eyes tightly. Pity and revulsion welled up inside him. A broken rope hung from a tree on the edge of the cliff, just above the ruined body below. He shuddered as he realized what must have happened. Even though he knew Judas had betrayed Jesus, his death was a tragic end.

"His story didn't *have* to end this way," said a voice quietly behind him. Peter inhaled sharply, came to his feet, and spun around. Jesus, the Son of God, alive once again, stood looking at him. Speechless, Peter stepped tentatively toward his rabbi. Jesus wrapped him tightly in his arms.

Sobs shaking his whole body, Peter laid his head on Jesus' shoulder. After a few seconds, he gasped, "I'm so sorry. I didn't mean to leave you. I was afraid." Jesus just tightened his embrace, patted him once or twice, and said, "I know."

Peter stepped back and wiped his eyes. Jesus placed his hands on Peter's shoulders and reminded him gently, "Satan has sifted you like wheat. But I have prayed for you, that your faith may not fail."

Jesus drew Peter closer to the dead body. He repeated, "His story didn't have to end this way. If he had repented, I would have forgiven him also." His eyes sought out Peter's, locked on. "Do you understand?"

Peter was thunderstruck. Jesus would have forgiven the man who had betrayed him, whom Jesus himself had called a devil, doomed to destruction?

Jesus added, "Even now, only my Father knows what was in Judas' heart during those last desperate few minutes of his life—his frantic dash to the Temple, his attempt to right that sin, the final run into the darkness. And his fate rests in my Father's hands."

Belatedly, Peter realized Jesus had said, "also." And twin truths crashed in on him—that he and Judas were both guilty, and that "also" meant Jesus *had* forgiven Peter, who had denied him publicly three times! He bowed his head, and tears ran down his cheeks anew.

Then Jesus said, "Come, Peter. I need your help." And together, the Forgiver and the forgiven lifted the corpse, carried it to a shallow grave nearby, and buried it.

As they worked, Jesus said, "'My Father is compassionate and gracious, slow to anger, abounding in love ... He does not treat us as our sins deserve or repay us according to our iniquities. As high as the heavens are above the earth, so great is his love for those who fear him; as far as the east is from the west, so far has he removed our transgressions from us.'"

Jesus paused until Peter looked at him, "Peter, you can be sure that these words are for you as well."

Reflect

1. Luke 24:34 says that Jesus appeared to Simon (Peter) before he appeared to the apostles that Resurrection Sunday night. Besides the possibility above, where else might Jesus and Peter have met that day? What did they say to each other?
2. Is there anything in your life that you think Jesus can't or won't forgive? Since Jesus did forgive Peter, and might have forgiven Judas, does that give you hope?

Learn

The Hinnom valley had a significant and often negative role in the history of Jerusalem (2 Chron. 28:3, 33:6, Jeremiah 7:31-35, and Jeremiah 19). It may also be connected to the stories of the potter in Jeremiah 18, 19, Zechariah 11:13, and Matthew 27:7-10.

Vignette 11

The Best Torah Lesson in History

Luke 24:13-35
(And see OT references from Jesus in the learning section.)

Cleopas and his wife Mary tarried to eat their Sunday lunch with the other disciples in the house. The momentous news the women had brought dominated the conversation. Even though the women were trustworthy, still—someone rising from the dead? It was too fantastic a leap to make.

Rising from the table, Cleopas and Mary said a quiet goodbye to the group and headed northwest out of Jerusalem for the seven-mile walk to their home in Emmaus.

Picking up the thread of the conversation from lunch, Mary insisted, "I know that everyone was exhausted by everything that happened this week, and by Jesus' death. But the women's story seems different—not like a dream or hallucination at all. They know Jesus. And Mary Magdalene said she saw Jesus himself—not just angels. They wouldn't lie to us."

Cleopas sighed. "I know. I can't imagine them lying, either. I want to believe it, but what if they were mistaken? What if someone did steal the body? Then wouldn't we want to go back to Jerusalem and help the disciples hunt for it?"

In the pause that followed his question, Mary and Cleopas heard steps behind them. They glanced back to see a man rapidly overtaking them.

The man joined them, saying, "Shalom!" Then he inquired, "What were you discussing together as you walked along?"

Cleopas and Mary hesitated, then slowed to a stop. Cleopas responded sadly, "Are you the only one visiting Jerusalem who does not know the things that happened there in these days?"

"What things?" he asked.

"About Jesus of Nazareth," Cleopas replied. "He was a prophet, powerful in word and deed before God and all the people. The chief priests and our rulers handed him over to be sentenced to death, and they crucified him, then buried him in a tomb."

Mary added, "We had hoped that he was the one who would redeem Israel."

Cleopas continued, "What's more, today is the third day since this took place. And this morning some of the women from our group amazed us. They went to the tomb early but didn't find his body. They came to the house and told us that they had seen a vision of angels, who said he was alive! Then, some of our friends went to the tomb and found it empty, as the women said. But they did not see Jesus."

The couple waited to see how the stranger might react. To their astonishment, his mouth curved in a rueful grin, and he shook his head slowly. "How foolish you are, and how slow to believe all that the prophets have spoken! Didn't the Messiah have to suffer these things and then enter his glory?"

Mary and Cleopas were bewildered and a little offended. Foolish? Slow to believe? They had followed the rabbi Jesus for years, to the bitter end. Yet—was this man affirming that their friend Jesus was the Messiah? Who was he to claim that with such authority?

"What do you mean?" asked Mary.

"You hear, but do not understand; you see, but do not perceive. If you truly saw and heard, then you might understand with your hearts."

The couple listened, chastened, but still confused. "We want to understand—could you please help us?"

The man gave them a warm smile. "It's a good beginning. Come, let's walk together."

He began, "You're right when you say Jesus was a prophet; in fact, he is the 'prophet like Moses' mentioned in Deuteronomy, to whom the people should listen.

"You've seen Jesus and what he did—but did you really *see* who he is? You have heard him teach—but did you really *hear* what he said?" A small smile played on the stranger's lips.

"What do Moses and the prophets say about the Messiah? A virgin would conceive and give birth, in the town of Bethlehem of Ephrathah. From this village that provides lambs for the Passover sacrifice would come the perfect Lamb; from these shepherds who tend the flocks, there would come a Shepherd with God's heart.

"Do you remember how, years ago, the mothers of Bethlehem cried out in anguish as Herod's soldiers killed their sons, just as Rachel cried for her sons? I tell you, at that time, the Messiah was a baby in Bethlehem, yet the Lord sent him and his parents safely to Egypt. Later, God called his son, the Messiah, out of Egypt on a second exodus from that land. The Messiah and his parents returned to a town whose name proclaims that one of their own would one day be the Branch that would bear fruit for the Lord.

"The Messiah would be the suffering Servant, on whom God would put his Spirit. He would mend broken reeds and nourish flickering flames. He would heal the blind, lame, and deaf, and liberate God's people from oppression of all kinds.

"He would feed people bread in the wilderness yet would also become the spiritual Bread by which people could live forever.

"Like the One who sent him, the Messiah would be the Rock in the desert from which living Water would flow for eternal life. He himself would sustain them until they reached the Promised Land. This Messiah would live among his people and be their King."

The stranger searched the faces of Mary and Cleopas as they recalled events and prophecies taught to them from infancy, yet they struggled to examine those prophecies through a new lens. Slowly, the ancient words of the Law and the Prophets acquired a different flavor as their perspective shifted. The Messiah promised in Scripture began to reveal himself and take on the face of Jesus. The miracles they had witnessed from Jesus gradually merged with the prophesied actions of the Messiah, the Anointed One, the Christ.

Mary and Cleopas' companion chuckled softly as he watched understanding dawn in their eyes, confirming, "Jesus is the Christ!"

As they approached Emmaus, their companion continued, "The prophet Zechariah said the Messiah would come to you, gentle and riding on a donkey. Do you remember anything like that during the last few days?"

Mary caught her breath.

The man added, "But Zechariah also said, 'righteous and having salvation.' What name comes from the word salvation?"

The couple answered in unison, "Jesus!"

He nodded.

"Zechariah later described how the sheep and the shepherd grew weary of each other, and the sheep gave the shepherd his pay to get rid of him—thirty pieces of silver! And eventually those thirty pieces of silver were thrown into the house of the Lord.

"Isaiah said the Messiah will be a stone that causes people to stumble and a rock that makes them fall. The Psalmist added that the stone the builders rejected has become the cornerstone."

He looked at them quizzically to see if they were catching his meaning.

"With a unified voice, every part of Scripture testifies that the Messiah must suffer these things and then enter his glory.

"In the Prophets, Isaiah called him a man of suffering, familiar with pain, wounded, pierced, crushed, a lamb led to slaughter.

"In the Law, Moses pictured him as the Passover lamb whose blood will protect God's people, as the scapegoat who receives all the sin of Israel and is banished outside the camp. As with the bronze serpent, the people would look upon the Messiah as he is lifted up, and they would be healed.

"In the Writings, the Psalmist described his anguish and said that the servant accuses God of forsaking him, refusing to answer him or save him. The people surround him, mock him, insult him, divide his clothes, and cast lots for them. Yet, the Psalmist also said that, in the eyes of God, the death of his holy one is precious and highly valued. And God would not let his holy one see decay."

Their companion gave them a penetrating look. "Do you now understand? Consider what your friend Jesus did this last week in light of what I have told you."

At that moment, Cleopas and Mary arrived at their small house on the outskirts of Emmaus. The stranger acted as if he would continue down the road, but Mary took hold of his sleeve. "Please—it's almost evening. It would be an honor if you would share our meal tonight."

He assented, and they entered the house and gathered around the table. Mary brought a simple meal of bread, olives, figs, and wine. Cleopas invited him to give the blessing before the meal.

Yet the man did not recite the traditional blessing. Rather, as if concluding the thoughts he shared on the road, he said, "Your friend Jesus was crucified on the cross at the same hour the priests sacrificed the Passover lamb in the Temple, for the nation of Israel. He died on the same mountain where God provided a sacrifice for Abraham, replacing his son Isaac.

"Jesus was taken from the cross and buried on the eve of the feast of unleavened bread—the day when people plant seeds of wheat and pray to God to provide bread from the earth to give life.

"And Jesus was raised from the dead by God on the day of harvest, the day when the first fruits come from the earth.

The stranger took the bread in his hands, lifted his face toward heaven, and prayed, "Blessed are you, Lord, King of the Universe, for providing this bread and life for us—now and forever."

He broke the bread and gave it to them. As they raised their heads, their eyes were truly opened. Expecting to see the stranger, they saw their Jesus! They gasped, wondering if it was a dream.

They cried out, "Jesus!" and rushed to embrace him, but he disappeared from their sight. They stared at each other, dazed, mouths ajar, looking first at his seat, then at each other, the same question in their eyes.

Cleopas asked Mary, "Was it real? Did you see him too?"

She responded, "I think so—my heart was burning within me as we listened to him on the road!"

With sudden certainty, they believed. They cried out at the same instant, "Let's go tell the others!" Reenergized, they ran out of the house, heading back to Jerusalem, knowing their world had changed forever.

Reflect

1. What other connections do you see in the Old Testament to Jesus and his ministry?
2. If Jesus is who he says he is—Son of God, Savior, Messiah, Lamb, Lord, and more—what kind of response do you think is appropriate for you?

Learn

Check out these possible Old Testament references from Jesus' lesson on the road.

After the Tomb

1. Moses speaks about the prophet Dt. 18:15
2. A virgin will conceive Is. 7:14
3. The Messiah to be born in Bethlehem Mic. 5:2
4. Shepherds of Bethlehem Lu. 2:8ff
5. Slaughter in Bethlehem, Mt. 2:16ff, Jr. 31:15
6. Jesus' family sent to Egypt Mt. 2:13-15
7. Second Exodus from Egypt Mt. 2:23
8. Hebrew word for Nazareth comes from *ntzer*, Branch Is. 11:1
9. Suffering Servant Is. 42:1ff
10. Mend reeds and nourish flames Mt. 12:20
11. All kinds of healing Lu. 4:18-19
12. Blind, deaf, lame Is. 35:5-6
13. Bread from heaven, Ex. 16, Mt. 14:14ff
14. Living by physical and spiritual bread Mt. 4:4, Dt. 8:3
15. Rock in the desert 1 Cor. 10:4, Ex. 17:1ff
16. The Hebrew word, *mashiach*, and the Greek word *Christos*, both mean "Anointed One."
17. King, gentle, riding on donkey Zc. 9:9, Mt. 21:5
18. Shepherd fired by sheep, 30 pieces of silver, Zc. 11:12ff, Mt. 27:5
19. Stone that causes people to stumble, Is. 8:14, Ps. 118:22-23Suffering Messiah Is. 53
20. Passover Lamb whose blood protects people Ex. 12:21ff
21. Scapegoat banished from the camp Lv. 16:20ff
22. Look on bronze serpent to be saved Nu. 21:9
23. Anguish on cross, forsaken by God Ps. 22
24. Precious is the death of the saints Ps. 116:15
25. Holy one wouldn't see decay, Ps. 16:10, Ac. 2:27
26. Near sacrifice of Isaac Gn. 22.

Also, see Ray Vander Laan's teaching on Jesus and the Jewish feasts.

https://www.thattheworldmayknow.com/jewish-feasts

Vignette 12

Who Are These People? (Part 1)

Matthew 27:51-53

Late Sunday afternoon, Thomas and Matthew had gone to the shops near the Temple Mount to purchase food for those staying at the house. They were conversing about the events of the morning, unable to sort out what might be true.

Thomas scoffed, "Really, how often does a person come back to life after three days?"

Matthew lifted an eyebrow and pursed his lips.

Thomas admitted, "All right. I know Lazarus was raised from the dead on the fourth day. But Jesus was the one who raised him. How is Jesus going to raise himself from the dead?"

Just then, a couple approached. Matthew noticed their clothes looked quite old, of a style he'd never seen before. The couple paused as they drew near to the two men.

Matthew greeted. "Shalom! Are you here for Passover?"

Their eyes sparkled. They seemed to be barely suppressing great excitement. "No! We just came into the city several hours ago."

Matthew asked, "Oh? Where are you from?

The couple glanced at each other, then the man declared, "We came from the tombs outside of town."

"You were visiting the grave of family or friends?" queried Thomas.

Looking intently at him, the man said quietly, "We were dead. In a tomb."

Matthew and Thomas stared at him, speechless.

"The last thing we remember was being very ill, in our family's home. The doctors had come but couldn't do anything. People were praying and weeping over us.

"The next thing we knew, we were awake in the tomb. We heard people shouting outside. We couldn't figure out what was happening, or exactly where we were. Since the stone sealing the tomb had broken into pieces, we ventured outside and looked toward the city. We thought it was Jerusalem, but—it was not like we remembered."

Thomas looked away and shook his head slightly.

The woman noticed and said, "I know it sounds crazy. We don't understand it yet ourselves."

Matthew asked, "Did this just happen today?"

"No," the man replied. "Two nights and days have passed. We've spent the last couple of days hiding out in the olive groves on the mountainside. Today we finally got up the courage to enter the city and wander around. The last time we had seen it, while we were still alive, it was smaller, with fewer buildings. And the Temple Mount and courtyard are much larger than we remembered.

"We asked someone if this was Jerusalem. They gave us a strange look and said, 'Of course!' When we asked them who was now king, they seemed exasperated and went on without answering us.

"Someone finally told us that the tetrarch of Galilee, Herod Antipas, was in town. They said that Tiberius was Caesar of the Roman Empire. When we asked them who the Romans were, those people also walked away."

Thomas objected, "How is it *possible* that you don't know about the Romans? Who did you expect to be king?"

The couple paused, certain that two more men were about to abandon them. "It may not make sense, but when we died, Hezekiah was king."

Thomas and Matthew squinted and cocked their heads at an angle but remained silent.

The woman shrugged, spreading out her hands slightly. "It's true! Somehow, God raised us to life. We're talking to everyone we can to find out what's happening. Can you tell us what's going on?"

Thomas turned abruptly to Matthew. "I need to get away from all this and think by myself. You take the food to the house. I'll come back later tonight." And he departed, heading toward the Garden of Gethsemane.

The couple waited to see if Matthew would answer them. Sighing, Matthew turned to them and said, "It's been an extremely unusual day, and honestly, we don't know what's going on either. Let me tell you a story."

Reflect

1. Have you ever seen or heard any class, sermon, article, book, or video about these holy people? Who might they have been? What did they do after they went into Jerusalem? Who else would they have appeared to?
2. How would you have responded to them in such a conversation?

Learn

The Bible leaves tantalizing holes in the "exit stories" of people like Enoch, Moses, Elijah, the son of the widow of Nain, Jairus' daughter, Lazarus, and the saints of Matthew 27:52. What can you learn about their deaths or exits and re-entries into the world? What might Romans 2:9 mean for them? Though it's written about Christ, the first fruits from the dead, could it also apply to these people?

Vignette 13
Celebration in Bethany

Luke 10:38-42; Psalm 27:4-14

Jesus turned onto the street where Lazarus, Mary, and Martha lived, calling out as he approached their house, "Mary! Martha! Lazarus!"

The brother and sisters were seated in the kitchen. When they heard the familiar voice, they froze for an instant. They had this very morning received the news that Jesus was alive and had been with his disciples. In fact, the siblings were about to head over to Jerusalem to see if they might find him.

The three bolted from their seats and met Jesus as he came through the door. He held his arms out wide and tried to embrace all three at once as tears, laughter, and wonder overflowed, erasing much of the heartbreak they had endured for the last three days.

They seated Jesus in the living room and gathered close around him, examining every detail of his face and his expressions, comforted and joyous at the sound of his voice as he told them about meeting the disciples the night before in the Jerusalem house.

His voice trailed off as he looked behind them, and his expression grew tender. Following his gaze, they looked around and saw his mother Mary, halted in the doorway to the bedroom, an incredulous look on her face.

Jesus went to her quickly. Her expression brightened, and her eyes shone. She reached out, took his face in her hands, and stood there, tears of joy trickling down her cheeks.

Jesus laid his hands on her shoulders and took a ragged breath. "Mother…"

She said, "My son."

For a while, nothing more needed to be said as they hugged each other.

Late that morning, the five of them gathered in the kitchen to prepare a simple lunch.

Jesus said to Martha, "Do you remember the first time I came to your home? You were so kind to invite me, so worried that every detail be right. Do you remember what you said to me?"

"Ha! I remember!" Mary interjected. "'Don't you care that my sister has left me to do the work by myself? Tell her to help me.'"

Martha admitted, "I did want her to help, but there were more than 20 people to feed."

Jesus smiled. "The Lord gave you the gift and desire to serve others, Martha. You have been faithful to use it—well done! Your example is a blessing to many."

Martha blushed. "That day, you told me that only one thing was truly necessary—to learn from you. I was slow to accept that."

Jesus nodded. "King David said, 'One thing I ask of the Lord … that I may dwell in the house of the Lord all the days of my life, to gaze upon the beauty of the Lord and to seek him in his Temple … my heart says of you, "Seek his face."'"

"Those who choose to seek the Lord, dwell in his presence, and learn from him as you have done, Mary, are also blessed. The Lord honors those who hope in him.

"What lies ahead for you three will not be easy. Lazarus, the Jews are seeking to kill you because of your testimony about your resurrection. All three of you are known to be my friends. Like David, you will be in danger from false witnesses, oppressors, and enemies. Like David, I tell you—be strong and take heart and wait for the Lord. He is your stronghold."

Their faces were solemn as they took in his words.

Martha suddenly said. "Look! Mary's in the kitchen helping me!" Mary rejoined, "And you're sitting here listening to Jesus!"

They laughed, took the food they had prepared, and gathered around the table, giving thanks to God together.

Reflect

1. How do you balance being with Jesus and handling the necessary tasks of life and ministry?
2. In your life, what has been the most useful way to sit with and learn from Jesus?

Learn

Who are all the different Marys in Jesus' life, and what did he do with them? I can think of possibly six.

VIGNETTE 14
THE INTRIGUING CASE OF LAZARUS

John 11; John 12:9-10; 2 Kings 2:11; Genesis 5:24

During lunch with Mary, Martha, and Lazarus, Jesus said, "Let me tell you a part of your story that you may not know. Lazarus, when I first heard that you were ill, my disciples and I were two days journey from here, across the Jordan." He paused.

Martha said, "Only two days! But ... you could have gotten here sooner, and ..." Her voice faded, and her eyes were troubled.

Jesus gazed at her, his eyes softening.

"You 're right. I could have ... but I waited two more days. I told the disciples Lazarus was asleep, and they were glad, thinking he would get better. So, I told them plainly that he was dead, and that for their sake, I was glad I was not with him."

There was an awkward silence as the three struggled to take this in. Then Lazarus ventured, "But, Jesus, we know you love us. How could you make my sisters wait? Why were you glad you weren't here? And because you didn't arrive in time ... I died." He dropped his gaze, hurt and confused.

They waited for Jesus to answer.

"I know it's hard to understand," he said gently. "My Father had a greater purpose in mind with you.

"Everyone believed I could heal because they had seen many miracles. But when I raised you from the dead, suddenly it was clear that *anything* was possible! The Jews recognize that, too, and for this reason want to silence you. If my disciples believe that my Father can deliver them even from death, nothing can stop them."

They pondered this for a moment, still unsure how to feel about it.

"Martha, you came to meet me when we arrived in Bethany. Bless you, for your faith in me then, in spite of your grief. You believed my Father could still give me whatever I asked. You also believed that Lazarus would rise again in the resurrection of the last day.

"You were thinking of the resurrection as a day, a time in the future—and in a way it is, of course. But I tell you that the resurrection is not a day; I myself *am* the resurrection. My very presence in my followers *is* life! My Father granted me authority to give life, and for three years, I did just that—feeding, healing, teaching, and raising from the dead.

"Eternal life is knowing me and receiving life in these ways and so many more. If you believe in me, you will never die permanently. Even if you pass through the gates of death, the life you began with me on this side of the grave will continue on the other side." He grinned at Lazarus. "Right, Lazarus?"

Lazarus nodded, "Now I understand more than I did. When people ask me about my resurrection, I tell them not just how I left the grave, but about the source of Life before and after my death. You wanted people to know that not only you could have this life, but that we could too."

Martha exclaimed, "So, when you asked me if I believed we would never die, you really meant that with you around, eternal life has already begun! I thought we had to wait for some moment in the future. When you declared I would see the glory of God, you meant *right then!*"

She recalled, with a voice full of wonder, "You simply said, 'Lazarus, come out,' and he did."

Mary turned to Lazarus, "What happened on your side of the grave? What were you doing when Jesus called you?"

Lazarus was still for a moment, lost in thought. "I remember a celebration, with beautiful music and laughter. We were at a long table, sharing the best food I've ever had—sorry, Martha—fruits I had never seen before, rich red wine, fresh hot bread, meats and spices—everything in abundance. Everything was brightly lit, though I didn't see any lamps.

"My parents were there, and my older brother, and family friends who had died long ago. All of them were young and strong and vibrant. Everyone was happy. No one was worried about what would happen the next day. No one complained about the Romans or the Zealots or Caesar. No one was sick or lame or needy. No one was arguing or angry or sad.

"The table where we were sitting seemed to be endless. There were people I had never met, but somehow I knew who they were—Abraham and Sarah, Ruth and Boaz, Elizabeth and Zechariah. Daniel was talking with Ezekiel, and Enoch with Methuselah, and so many more.

"I had always wanted to ask them questions, and now I could. I got up from my place and started walking toward them—then I heard a voice I recognized. 'Lazarus! Come out!'"

He looked down, then over at Jesus, and was surprised to see that Jesus had a tear in his eye. Lazarus turned back to Mary. "So, I left them and came back." He shrugged. "I love all of you, and these days since the grave have been dear to me, but ... I was a little sad to return." Mary searched his eyes deeply, then wrapped her arms around her brother and held him tightly.

After Mary, Martha, and Jesus' mother said goodbye to Jesus, Lazarus strolled with him back down the road to Jerusalem. Lazarus said, "Those few moments in heaven stirred in me the desire to be there always. You must have had a reason for calling me back. I know I'm to be a witness for you here, and I'll gladly do that. But what will happen to me now? Will the Jews succeed in killing me? Should I go somewhere else to testify?"

Jesus sighed. "Part of me didn't want to bring you back, because I know the perfect life my Father has waiting for everyone who believes in him. I've lived it too. I helped create it! And I look forward to returning to it.

"Yet you're an important part of my Father's plan to teach people what he is preparing for them in heaven if they will believe. You've *seen* it. Your faithfulness is bringing great joy in heaven, and my Father has stored up a reward for you."

Overwhelmed by the answer, Lazarus slowed to a stop. Jesus studied his face as Lazarus tried to absorb the words. He hesitated, then asked the question that had been weighing on his mind, "Since I already died and came back to life, will I not die ever again? Will I be here till the judgment day? Or will God carry me to heaven one day, like Elijah or Enoch?"

Jesus smiled. "For right now, that's one of the answers that only the Father knows. However, speaking of people who have been resurrected to live here again, I have a favor to ask of you, my friend.

"Last Friday, many holy people were raised to life after I died, and yesterday they went into the city. They were amazed and incredulous. They walked around and talked to whoever they found. I don't know who was more confused—them or the people they met." Jesus chuckled. "I'm afraid Thomas had a hard time with it.

"Now they don't know what to do. They have no families to take them in, only the clothes on their backs, no jobs or income. Will you and your sisters give them food and lodging for a time in your home, until they're able to find what they need?"

"Of course we will. It would be an honor!" responded Lazarus. "But will they want to stay with us?"

"I imagine they'd be delighted. After all, who else in all Jerusalem would understand their experience? You've lived it too. In fact—you'll recognize some of them who were at the banquet table with you in heaven before you were called back to earth. They followed you back to earth shortly afterward."

Reflect

1. What do you think Lazarus did in heaven before Jesus called him back? How might his life change once he returned from the grave?
2. If you are a follower of Jesus, you have eternal life in you; in a way, eternal life has already begun for you. Which parts of your life right now are eternal, and which are temporary?

Learn

For an interesting take on the story and resurrection of Lazarus, I recommend Bodie and Brock Thoene's book, *When Jesus Wept* (Jerusalem Chronicles, book 1, especially pp. 263ff).

Vignette 15

An Unforgettable Walk to Bethlehem

Luke 2:19, 22-38; Genesis 16, 21; John 8:1-11

Early the next morning, Jesus met his mother, Mary at the pool of Siloam. From there, they set out toward Bethlehem, about five and a half miles south of Jerusalem.

The tragedy of just four days before melted away in the rising sun. As they walked, Mary found herself often looking up at Jesus, as if to reassure herself that this was not a dream, that she would not wake up at Martha's house on Friday night, desolate and wretched.

And it was not a dream!

The fresh morning air cooled them, the flowers along the road were brightly colored, and the birds sang cheerily, as if, at least for a time, creation had been set right again. Jesus and Mary laughed as they reminisced about Jesus' childhood in Nazareth.

Jesus asked her, "Mother, you've told me the story of going to the Temple and conversing with Anna and Simeon. You said once, 'That was one of the memories I stored up like treasures in my heart.' Please, what are some of the other treasures?"

Mary recalled, "Bedtimes! On summer nights, Joseph, you, and I would go up on the roof of our little house. We would roll out our mats and lie down together, look up at the stars, sing songs, tell stories, and listen to the sounds of the night, the gentle breeze cooling us off after a hot day.

"One night, when you were about eight years old, Joseph was telling how God faithfully kept his promise to Abraham, Sarah, and Isaac, and how amazing it must have been to have a child when they were so old.

"That night you seemed distracted, almost sad. I asked you, 'Is something wrong?' and you said, 'My Father was sad about that.' We asked, 'Sad about what?'

"You said, 'That Sarah and Hagar couldn't get along, and that Hagar was sent away. My Father watched over Hagar and Ishmael, grieving, from the moment they left Abraham's tent till their water ran out. But when they were about to die, Father sent Michael to Hagar to show them water, and where to go next.'

"Your father and I were astonished. As casually as we could, we asked, 'Jesus, how did you know that about God and Hagar?'

"And you said, 'I was there with my Father, watching over her.'

"Goosebumps swept over us. It was as if we were briefly in another place, with angels around us, and we were reminded that you were a special gift to us from God."

Mary laughed softly. "That's one of my treasures."

"I remembered that story," Jesus affirmed. "Not just that night, but all during my ministry. How my Father felt about Hagar is how he feels about everyone who is cast out, shunned, or vulnerable."

He asked, "Do you remember the morning I was teaching in the Temple, and the leaders brought me the woman they had trapped in adultery?"

She nodded, "I felt sorry for her, even though what she did was wrong."

Jesus reached out and hugged her tenderly. "You're just like my Father," he said quietly.

"So, when I saw that woman, I thought of Hagar, cast out,

thrown down, hopeless, resigned to death." He walked in silence for a while. "Like my Father, I see the Hagars all around us—people guilty of some kind of sin, whom others want to punish. But their accusers are also guilty, just like Abraham and Sarah and the Jewish leaders were. There aren't enough rocks to throw ..."

His voice trailed off. "But my Father isn't interested in throwing rocks. He'd rather offer a second chance at life."

Reflect

1. In Luke 2 (vv. 19 and 51), it says Mary treasured these things in her heart. What are other things you believe she would treasure from all her experiences as the mother of Jesus?
2. If someone asked you what personal experiences with Jesus you treasure, what would they be?

Learn

Read the chapter "25 Questions for Mary" in Max Lucado's book, *God Came Near.* W Publishing Group, 2007.

Vignette 16
Tragedy in Bethlehem, Revisited

Matthew 2:1-18

The news that Jesus and Mary were in Bethlehem at Joseph's family's cave spread like wildfire. Several long-time family friends came to the cave to see them and hear Jesus' incredible story.

After he finished, the conversation naturally turned to the past. Salmon and Ruth's family had been in Bethlehem for centuries. In fact, they claimed Boaz and Ruth as their ancestors. Jesse and Deborah traced their lineage back to an earlier Jesse, the father of King David. Two of the families there had suffered through Herod's terrible purge when soldiers had slaughtered all the male children less than two years old.

"We remember the night you gave birth, Mary," said Ruth. "We hoped that you and Joseph might decide to stay here and not go back to Nazareth."

Jesse added, "Those first few months were a blessed time. Our little Isaac was born just three months before you, Jesus. Salmon and Ruth had six-month-old Obed. We worshiped together in the synagogue, worked in the fields, and watched our sons play, dreaming about them growing strong in the years to come.

"Then one day, a procession of camels appeared in Bethlehem with several distinguished men who said they had come from the East to visit the new king. We were baffled. We didn't know about any king in our little village. But they went straight to your house to see Jesus. No family in Bethlehem had ever received such presents!"

Ruth added, "It was a mystery. How did these men know about you or the baby? Why did they call Jesus a king? Why those expensive gifts? I can tell you, it gave us a lot to talk about for the next few days."

"Then suddenly, you and Joseph and Jesus were gone," said Salmon. "No one in the village knew what had happened. Some thought you had gone back to Nazareth. Others thought maybe you went to your parents' house in Sepphoris, Mary."

"And then we all forgot those questions," said Deborah, "because one night Herod's soldiers charged into Bethlehem, demanding to see the new king who had been born. Again, we were confused. We hadn't understood when the men from the East talked about a king, and we still didn't."

Salmon shook his head. "We tried to tell the soldiers we didn't know anything, but they thought we were lying to them to protect the king. So, their leader threatened us. 'If you won't tell us, we'll kill *all* the baby boys under two years old!'

"We were horrified! The soldiers tore through the village, smashing doors, invading houses. Every time they found a baby boy, they would run him through with a sword, or dash him against the stones in the streets. We were out of our minds, desperate to save our children. One soldier slashed Jesse and knocked him down, and another hit me on the head with his shield and knocked me out."

Silence lingered in the cave, broken only by sobs as each replayed that dreadful night in his or her head. Thirty years had not dulled their pain and anger. Jesus and Mary exchanged a sober glance, struck afresh by the tragic suffering of their friends.

After the Tomb

Salmon resumed the story. "When I woke up, the soldiers were gone. From every house and cave in the village, weeping and anguished cries emerged. We had lost Obed, and Jesse and Deborah lost little Isaac." He took a deep, ragged breath. "It took us a long time to recover from that." His wife Ruth nodded, dabbing at her eyes.

"But the Lord was gracious to us all," Salmon continued. "Most of the families who lost their babies had more children later. Of course, we never forgot those boys, and we always wondered what they might have become, but the children we still had were a great comfort to us."

Ruth smiled at Mary. "What a blessing that Jesus was not here—at least you all avoided the purge."

At this, Mary and Jesus didn't seem relieved, but rather burdened. Mary told them quietly, "There's a part of the story the families in Bethlehem have never heard. Soon after the magi visited us, Joseph was warned in a dream that Herod would search for Jesus to try to kill him. The angel told us to flee to Egypt. So that very night, desperate to protect Jesus, we packed what little we could and left for Egypt."

Mary faced Ruth and Deborah. "It never crossed our minds what might happen here. We felt certain that if Herod came and didn't find Jesus, he would just look somewhere else. We never imagined that his soldiers would make the rest of the village suffer.

"When we heard what happened, we felt so guilty. Our son was the one Herod wanted to kill, but your innocent babies died." Mary bowed her head and wiped a tear from her eye. "We never knew what to say to anyone. It wasn't our fault, yet that's the main reason we haven't visited here for so long."

Mary knelt at the feet of Ruth and Deborah. "We are so sorry that you all lost your precious babies. Joseph and I felt terrible about it for years. Can you ever forgive us?"

Jesse, Deborah, Ruth, and Salmon looked at Mary and Jesus, then at each other, tears slowly coursing down their cheeks. The wounds had been ripped open again by this new part of the story. Yet how could they blame Mary and Joseph? Anyone might have done the same. Wordlessly, they stretched out their arms to Mary and Jesus, and the deep wounds of decades began to heal.

Reflect

1. Do you think that during his ministry, Jesus ever taught or healed anyone from Bethlehem who was part of that tragic night?
2. Why did God select the Magi to visit Jesus? Besides blessing Jesus, did he have a purpose for them after they went back to their country?
3. How do you react to tragedies that it seems God could have prevented?

Learn

Some have suggested that the Magi came from a line of wise men and magicians descended from the prophet Daniel in Babylon and that he may have been the one who told them to watch the skies for signs of the new King of the Jews. Could the magi have carried the early gospel story to their homes as early missionaries, in a sense?

Vignette 17
Jesus Confronts Caiaphas

Matthew 28:11-15; John 5:31-47; Matthew 26:59-67; Hebrews 7:23-28

Back in Jerusalem Wednesday morning, Jesus strolled through the streets, picking up a light lunch at a place he and the apostles had visited in the lower city. He paused to share with a beggar outside the southwestern gate of the Temple, then went up the staircase leading into the Temple courts near the Royal Stoa. Once in the courts, he climbed the stairs by the Chamber of Hewn Stone, where the Sanhedrin often met.

As Jesus entered the Chamber, Caiaphas was instructing several Sadducees about Temple matters. The men soon left the Chamber. Jesus approached from behind Caiaphas, stopped, and said, "Caiaphas."

Caiaphas turned quickly, startled and somewhat irritated that someone would approach him unsolicited in this place. When he saw Jesus, his mouth fell open and the blood drained from his face.

"Caiaphas," Jesus repeated. "You've paid soldiers to spread a rumor that my body was stolen, and that I was still dead."

Caiaphas finally found his voice and sputtered, "You're a ghost! We killed you! Is this some sort of trick?"

Jesus shook his head. "You've lied about me and refused to believe in me for years. Your unbelief has caused many to stumble and reject me—your priests, the Sadducees, the Pharisees.

"According to the Law, every matter must be proved by the testimony of two or three witnesses. My Father chose as his witnesses himself, Moses, the Scriptures, the prophets, John the Baptizer, my works, and me. Seven witnesses who agreed in their testimony were clearly presented to you—and you ignored or rejected them all!

"In the sham trial you held for me, you could not find any witnesses who told the truth, and the two you did find gave flawed witness. Yet, because it was indeed my Father's will that one man must perish instead of the nation, I myself chose to testify before the Sanhedrin that I am the Messiah, the Son of Man.

"You called for the council to condemn me for blasphemy. You thought I was lying, that I was not the Messiah, and that you could be rid of me once and for all. Yet it was not blasphemy, because it was the truth. I *am* the Truth, standing alive once again before you."

Caiaphas' knees became weak. He clutched at a chair beside him and shakily lowered himself into it. He looked wildly around the room, seeking someone to wake him from this nightmare. Yet there was no relief, and he had no answer.

"You wondered how the curtain to the Most Holy Place was torn. I tell you that it was my Father, tearing the curtain as a man tears his tunic, in lament. At the same moment, my Father anointed me as eternal High Priest. Through me, all nations can now enter the Most Holy Place, at any time—not just one man on one day each year.

"You and those who come after you in this role will serve as assistants who answer to the true High Priest. Soon, Jerusalem's enemies will encircle the city and destroy it. Then there will be no human high priest to rule. Yet I will serve forever as High Priest for

After the Tomb

all those who choose to come to the Father through me because the Father has transferred all authority to me.

"You dared to judge and kill the Son of God. In the future, the risen Son will judge you. You must decide whether you will yet believe the witnesses my Father has provided you. Choose wisely."

With this final warning, Jesus turned and strode from the Chamber.

Reflect

1. How do you think Caiaphas' role and ministry changed after he discovered Jesus was alive? Do you think he became a believer?
2. Have you ever put yourself in the position of judging Jesus or misunderstood your relationship to him (on purpose or not)?

Learn

Study a good map of Herod's Temple and courts in Jesus' time, including the Chamber of Hewn Stone, where the Sanhedrin met. This will benefit enormously your understanding of Jewish customs and inform how you read several biblical stories that took place there. Leen Ritmeyer has an excellent detailed PowerPoint called, "Worship and Ritual in Herod's Temple," on his Ritmeyer archaeological design site.

https://www.ritmeyer.com/product-category/presentations/

Vignette 18

The "Man from the Dream" Visits Pilate and Procla

Matthew 27:11-26; John 18:33-40; Romans 6:9-10

Pilate was in his chambers at the Antonia Fortress. After the confusing trial last Friday, life was finally returning to normal. These Jews were irritating and unpredictable. He couldn't wait to finish this posting and be transferred to another city. Anywhere would be better than here.

Pilate's wife, Procla, entered the room, carrying a tray with figs, nuts, bread, and wine. She had been strangely reticent since the weekend, ever since he sentenced the Jewish rabbi to death. She set the tray on a table nearby without looking at him.

"Are you still stewing about that prisoner?" he barked. "I had no choice. If we had not crucified him, these Jews would have rioted, and Augustus Caesar won't tolerate uprisings. I'm afraid that the troubles of the last two years have already caused him to doubt me." He waited for her reaction.

Procla slowly lifted her eyes to meet his. "I know you're right. Yet, I've been troubled ever since the dream I had about him. He was not like Barabbas. He didn't seem to be rebelling against Rome." She appealed to him, "You thought the same. If it hadn't been for the Jewish leaders, wouldn't you have released him?"

"Perhaps," he admitted. "But it's too late now. He's dead and buried. When the Passover days end this week and most of the Jews go home, maybe we can finally put this behind us."

She ventured, "Please don't be angry, but have you heard the rumors the last several days? Some are saying that the rabbi came back to life and has been seen with his disciples."

Pilate snorted and shook his head. "Impossible. Just wishful thinking from his disciples and weak-minded people who'll believe anything." He stopped as the door opened.

Procla gasped. There stood the man from her dream! She darted a glance at Pilate.

He was staring at the man also, frozen with doubt and fear. Was he going crazy? Was the man a ghost?

"Greetings, Procla," said Jesus. "Don't be afraid. You spoke truly about me. Pilate, why didn't you believe her?"

Pilate, still struggling with the shock of seeing this man alive and well only five days after his trial and death, had no ready answer. Even if by some miracle, Jesus had not actually died, he certainly could not have recovered this quickly from the terrible wounds inflicted on him.

"I am no threat to either of you," Jesus assured them. "At least not in the ways you suppose. Pilate, when I told you that my kingdom is not of this world, I spoke the truth. I do not seek to take your place, nor that of Augustus.

"My kingdom is much bigger than Rome. My Father has given me authority over this entire world because I have honored and obeyed him. In fact, my kingdom extends beyond this world to the heavens.

"Not only that, my kingdom will never end. Long after this generation and future generations have lived and died, my kingdom will still flourish, and no one will ever defeat it.

"Now that I have triumphed over the last enemy, death, nothing, and no one has power over me. Rather, my Father has given all power to me.

"You worried about being held responsible for my death, and you washed your hands. You will indeed be held responsible for it. Yet you are not alone in that. Ultimately, my Father and I were the ones who foresaw and brought about my death, though many took part in it—Caiaphas, Herod, the Jews, you, your Roman soldiers, even humanity itself. All are liable in some way.

"You freed Barabbas, though you knew he was guilty, and I died instead of him. Now my Father and I offer you the same mercy. Though you are guilty of sin, we will forgive you, because you didn't know what you were doing.

"If you accept this, it will be costly to you, because in joining my kingdom, your allegiance will be first to me, rather than the Emperor. You will lose your privileged position, be ridiculed, and eventually charged with treason to the Empire. Even if you forfeit your life, you will gain eternal life in my kingdom.

"You asked me on Friday, 'What is truth?' What I am proclaiming to you is the truth, because I *am* the Truth. If you are on the side of truth, you will listen to me—and act on it."

REFLECT

1. What do you think this conversation between Pilate and Jesus might have covered? Could Pilate have been part of the early church movement later in Rome?
2. In the Gospels, Pilate seems reluctant to punish Jesus, yet eventually gives in to pressure from the Jews. Has there

been a time when pressure from others or some aspect of society led you to actions you later regretted?

Learn

The Wikipedia article on Pontius Pilate shows the wide variety of beliefs regarding his life, role in Jesus' crucifixion, and Pilate's own death, as well as the archaeological evidence concerning him, and mentions of him in various writings through the centuries, Christian and otherwise. Speculation about his later life ranges from the idea that he became a Christian, to the thought that he went mad and committed suicide.

VIGNETTE 19
WHO ARE THESE PEOPLE? (PART 2)

Acts 12:12-13; Mark 14:51; Matthew 27:52-53

Jesus awoke just before sunrise, having slept among the olive trees in the Garden of Gethsemane. He stood and watched as the white limestone of the Temple began to shine brilliantly in the early morning sun cresting the Mount of Olives.

As the city came to life, Jesus strode across the Kidron Valley, passed through the eastern gate into the Temple courts, and then out the western gate to the Tyropoeon Valley. He made his way to a house in the Lower City and knocked on the door. A young woman opened it, and Jesus greeted her, "Shalom, Rhoda!"

Her eyes opened wide, and she hugged him. "Rabbi! Come in!" She turned to the group assembled there eating breakfast.

A boy about twelve years old ran up to Jesus and hugged him. "Hello, Mark!" Jesus exclaimed, giving the boy a broad smile. He noticed the boy seemed embarrassed or a little sad. Jesus knelt and studied the boy's face. "What's wrong?"

The boy looked down at the floor. "I'm sorry I ran away from you … in the garden." He raised his eyes timidly to Jesus' face.

"I was glad you were safe." Jesus gave him a warm smile. "I didn't want to lose a single one of my friends that night." He hugged the boy again, then stood up as a woman hurried out from the back of the house and rushed straight to greet Jesus, kissing him on both cheeks. "Mary!" he said. "I'm so glad to see you again!"

He turned and surveyed the group of people gathered in the living room. "I see some guests have arrived." Mary took the cue. Laying a hand on Jesus' shoulder, she announced to the group, "This is Jesus, the man we've been telling you about. Last Friday afternoon, he died on a Roman cross. But then, on Sunday, God raised him from the dead, and we saw him that day.

"It's hard to believe, but of all people, I know this group can accept Jesus' resurrection, because that same Friday afternoon, his death literally freed you from the grave. Now you're privileged to meet the One responsible for your resurrection. He is the Resurrection and the Life."

The group listened to Mary intently with solemn faces. As she finished, there was a reverent silence, and one of the older men said, "Lord, we will serve you however you wish." One by one, the group knelt before him and bowed their heads. Jesus moved among them, laying his hands in blessing on their heads and shoulders. Then he gathered them around him in a circle.

"You've been called back to this world for a special purpose. I know you've been talking to each other about your experiences during these days and from your lives before. What have you learned about each other?" He looked at them expectantly.

One man ventured, "We seem to be from different times and places. My wife and I participated in the dedication of the Temple with Solomon."

Others chimed in.

"We were with Samuel the day Saul became king."

"My family helped Hezekiah build his tunnel and the wall around Jerusalem."

"We lived in Jerusalem after coming back from the exile in Babylonia."

"Our people crossed the Jordan with Joshua and marched around Jericho with him."

"We were some of the faithful remnant, along with Elijah, during Ahab's time."

"We were teenagers who survived forty years in the desert while waiting to reach the Promised Land."

"Our judge was Deborah. We helped defeat Sisera."

"We grew up in the land of Goshen while Joseph was still ruler of Egypt."

"As servants in the household of Abraham, when he rescued Lot; we met Melchizedek outside of Salem.

Jesus nodded. "So, can you guess what your mission might be?"

A woman responded, "It seems that together, we represent God's people since the time of Abraham."

"Exactly!" affirmed Jesus. "Though none of you have lived the whole story, each of you have witnessed key events in Israel's history. You have received my Father's promises, heard the prophets predict the coming of the Messiah, and have seen God's power, steadfast love, and faithfulness in multiple ways.

"And now you see me, the Messiah, the climax and the center of God's plan. Every promise God made is "Yes" in me in some way. I now send you now as witnesses together, to help people believe in me.

"During this time, you'll live with Lazarus, Mary, and Martha. They're expecting you. Each day, you'll go out from there to tell your story. You can talk with Lazarus about your mission here and about your time in heaven.

"And when your mission is finished, my Father will take you to himself again, much as he did with Elijah."

Reflect

1. Whom would these people have sought out to talk to when they first entered Jerusalem? What else would they do?
2. Would you believe someone with a similar story today? What would it take to convince you?

Learn

Read about the various historical periods represented by the people:

- Solomon and dedication of temple (I Ki. 8)
- Saul anointed (1 Sam. 10:24ff)
- Hezekiah's kingship (2 Chron. 32:1-5)
- Exiles returned (Ezra 2:1ff)
- Crossing the Jordan with Joshua (Josh. 3)
- Faithful remnant with Elijah (I Ki. 19:18)
- Teenagers in the desert (Num. 14:29ff)
- Deborah's army (Judg. 4:14ff)
- Land of Goshen (Gen. 4:5ff)
- Servants of Abraham (Gen. 14:14-24)

Vignette 20
Return to Golgotha

John 19:17-30; Psalm 30:3,5; Luke 2:35; John 10:17-18

On Friday, one week after his crucifixion, Jesus and his mother left the Temple after morning prayers and retraced the path Jesus took to the cross just seven days before. Jesus said, "Last Friday, this walk seemed to last forever—every inch laced with pain, the cross scraping and grinding on my back, heavier with each step, the soldiers lashing me when I would stumble and fall, sweat and blood blurring my vision, angry faces and jeering voices ...

"For my Father, it was the terrible climax of his plan since before this world was created. Just as I moved slowly walking to Golgotha, through the centuries, he moved slowly but steadfastly toward this moment. The world he had created mocked and rejected him at every turn, causing him pain and suffering, wanting to get rid of him so they could pursue other gods. Yet, in spite of the pain and rejection, he remained committed to his plan.

"You and my second father, Joseph, knew some of this pain since the day you spoke with Anna and Simeon in the Temple. Yet you also patiently believed and obeyed, playing your part in the plan, even when you didn't understand how things would work out. So, my Father, you, Joseph, and I were united in this walk to the cross, and none of us turned back.

"During my ministry, when people misunderstood, rejected, and mistreated me, you were always there, just like my Father. When I went to my trial, and the soldiers spit on me and scourged me, you and my Father shared in my pain. And you were standing at the foot of the cross, though for a time I felt my Father had forsaken me.

"As we walk this path again today, I know the pain returns." He glanced at her with a sober expression. "But I promise you that when you think about these events in the future, my Father will remind you of the unique bond you share with him. He will reward you with the joy of knowing that your faithfulness helped achieve his plan in bringing salvation to the world."

They passed through the Gennath Gate at the western edge of the city. Ahead was the old stone quarry, the killing ground of Golgotha. The taunts of the chief priests seemed to echo, "Let this Messiah, this king of Israel, come down now from the cross, that we may see and believe ..." The cross still lay on the ground, but the Messiah was now standing.

Jesus proclaimed in a ringing voice, "Today, this Scripture is fulfilled: 'You, Lord, brought me up from the realm of the dead ...Your anger lasts only a moment, but your favor lasts a lifetime. Weeping may remain for the night, but rejoicing comes in the morning.'" Jesus smiled. "*This* morning. And now his favor lasts forever."

They retraced the path from the cross to the tomb, ducked their heads to enter, and sat down, strangely comforted despite the recent raw memories.

Mary looked at the stone shelf. Last Friday had felt like the end of everything—life, happiness, hope. The darkness of the grave shrouded the present and the future.

"I felt ... crushed," she murmured. "None of it made sense. It didn't seem possible or real. I was trapped in a nightmare that just got worse, with no way out. And I was angry. Those hypocrites—Caiaphas and the priests! And Pilate ... only worried about his skin, freeing an assassin while he whipped and condemned my son."

Tears gathered in her eyes, though the son whom she saw die was now beside her, alive and compassionate, arm wrapped around her. "And I admit it ... I was *angry* with God too. I didn't understand why it all happened when we had both done what He wanted.

"One of the worst moments was when the soldiers came up and pierced your side with a lance. Why? You were already dead. It was as if a sword had pierced my soul. At that moment, I remembered what Simeon had said. I felt I would never recover from it."

Her eyes were bright with tears, the wounds still painful. Jesus tightened his grip and smiled tenderly at her. Sighing, she laid her head on his shoulder. The birds chirped outside the tomb and a soft breeze caressed Mary's face, as if to wipe away her tears. A profound peace warmed her heart, and she began to let go of her anger and sadness, as she realized that her son was back from the grave forever.

From outside came the sound of someone approaching the grave. A man entered the tomb, then jumped back with a startled cry as he saw them there, as if he thought they were ghosts. At the same instant, Mary and the man recognized each other—he was the centurion from the cross. Mary drew in a sharp breath, her eyes narrowed, and her lips clamped down into a straight line. "What are *you* doing here?" she demanded.

The centurion was distraught and rattled. He stammered, "I just came to check the tomb. Caiaphas is still furious, and Pilate is confused." He took a deep breath and looked at Jesus, bewildered. "Sir," he said respectfully, "is it really true? Did you ... were you ... well, I know you were dead, but we had to check."

Mary made a noise and glared at him. Instantly, he was ashamed, realizing she was angry about that very action.

He rushed on, "During these past few days, certain people claimed to have seen you, but we were skeptical. I came here to try to understand what happened."

With a patient smile, Jesus said, "Longinus, I believe you know what happened, don't you? My Father revealed part of the truth to you last Friday afternoon. You yourself said I must be the Son of God. And you were correct."

The centurion gazed at his face, mesmerized. Understanding dawned in his eyes as he realized that he had helped kill the Son of God. He lowered his head, weighed down by guilt.

He said in a low voice, "That day was so confusing. Nothing that happened was like any other crucifixion I'd ever done. Usually, the prisoner is clearly guilty. He's always desperate, angry, crying. But you seemed at peace, almost as if you, not Pilate, were the one in charge.

"None of it seemed right—the people mocking you or the soldiers taunting you with the vinegar, then gambling for your robe. I felt guilty the whole time. But I am a Roman centurion, and I was convinced I had to obey orders."

Jesus said, "Even though Caiaphas and Pilate sentenced me, and you nailed me to the cross, none of you really knew what you were doing. My Father gave me authority to lay my life down and to take it up again. And I also obeyed, so that I might give life to others.

"What you all did, Satan meant for evil, but God intended it for good, to save many lives. That's why, at that moment, I asked my Father to forgive you all."

The centurion lifted his eyes slowly to Jesus' face. The sincerity and compassion he saw there convicted and broke him. He sank to his knees before Jesus and put his forehead to the ground. He reached out and grasped Jesus' feet, his body convulsing with sobs. Jesus knelt by him and laid a gentle hand on his shoulder, waiting as the Spirit worked to heal the soldier's broken spirit.

Eventually the centurion raised his head off the ground and sat up. He declared again, this time with heartfelt gratitude and conviction, "Truly, you *are* the Son of God."

Jesus wrapped him in an embrace.

Mary watched, gripped by a storm of conflicting emotions. This man had tortured and crucified her son, causing her suffering as well. How could Jesus forgive him so calmly? Part of her wanted to follow Jesus' lead, but the memories were still too overwhelming.

The centurion finally stood and said to Jesus, "I have something to give you." He opened his pack lying nearby, rummaging inside while Jesus and Mary waited. Then he pulled out something, turned around, and held it out to Jesus.

Mary took a step closer to see what it was, and gasped. It was Jesus' robe—the one the soldiers had stolen from him as a gambling prize. She reached out and tentatively took it from Jesus' hands, noting with sadness the bloodstains still on it. With the robe clutched in her hands, her mind went back to a scene three years before.

Jesus had come in one night from his little shop near the house and joined her for their nightly supper and conversation. He had said, "I must leave soon to visit my cousin John, who is preaching near the Jordan. After that, I'll come back to Galilee, but I'll be living in Capernaum and teaching in all the synagogues of Galilee." He concluded gently. "It's time—I must be about my Father's business."

The next day, she began to make this robe. As she worked, she prayed over every inch of it. She invested love in every stitch and asked the Father to keep her son safe. He had worn this soft, beautiful reminder of his mother's love during his entire ministry—teaching, healing, walking, eating. When the soldiers stole it from him at the foot of the cross, it had been yet another painful blow.

Mary became aware that Jesus and Longinus were watching her.

She slowly faced the centurion. She was still hurt and angry, but holding this robe in her hands seemed to challenge her to follow her son's example. She looked at Longinus, and he returned the gaze, saying softly, "I am truly sorry for hurting your son, and for hurting you. I know I don't deserve it, but…can you ever forgive me?"

He waited as she studied his face. Jesus nodded encouragingly. She wondered if he had brought her here today partly to reconcile with the centurion. She suddenly perceived that as much as the centurion needed forgiveness, she needed to forgive, so she also might be healed.

Mary gave the robe to Jesus, then took a step toward the centurion and gripped his hands in hers. She looked him squarely in the eyes and said with certainty, "I do forgive you from my heart." As the words left her mouth, she realized with surprise that they were true. She suddenly felt lighter, as much of the sadness, anger, and lingering despair were banished. The centurion bit his lip, and tears welled up in his eyes. Speechless, he leaned forward and embraced her gently.

Jesus murmured, "Thank you, Father!"

Reflect

1. The centurions in the New Testament were remarkably open to God—a God-fearer like Cornelius, the one who helped build the Capernaum synagogue, and even the one on Paul's journey to Rome, who gave him favorable treatment. What might have happened to them after their encounters with God? Why do you think they were so receptive?

2. Forgiving can be extremely difficult for any of us. What might be preventing you from forgiving others in your life?

Learn

Many fiction books, loosely based on the biblical text, have been written about Jesus' ministry and death. An interesting one is called *The Robe* by Lloyd Douglas, which imagines the story of the centurion who crucified Jesus, before and after the event.

Vignette 21

A New Vision for Bartimaeus

Acts 8:39; Matthew 11:2-6; Matthew 9:27-31

Early Monday morning, Jesus left Jerusalem, heading northeast. Once on his way, the Spirit snatched him up and quickly placed him just outside the ancient city of Jericho, near a man tending a grove of fig trees outside a small house.

"Shalom!" Jesus hailed him.

The man turned slowly to return the greeting, then his face broke into an unbelieving smile, and he ran to Jesus to embrace him warmly.

"The first face I ever saw!" he bubbled. "Welcome to my humble home, Jesus."

Jesus smiled as he saw Bartimaeus' clear brown eyes. "It's good to see you again—and to be seen by you."

"Come in, come in," urged Bartimaeus. The two men settled down to talk.

"It's only been two weeks," said Jesus, "but it seems like longer. Tell me about what's happened since that day."

Ever irrepressible, Bartimaeus eagerly complied. "It was the most exciting day of my life. I had heard about you for two years and about how you were teaching and healing people all over Galilee. I wanted to go find you, but no one would go with me. It's dangerous for a blind man to travel alone, and easy for people to take advantage of him.

"I tried to be content with the stories that arrived here in Jericho. One of John's disciples passed through and stopped near my house to eat a meal with a friend. I listened as well as I could outside the door, hoping to be invited in. He said that he and other disciples had gone to visit you to ask if you were 'the one who was to come.'"

Bartimaeus smiled. "I knew they couldn't ask you directly if you were 'the Messiah.' That could get everyone in trouble with the Pharisees and the Romans. And you couldn't answer directly, either.

"So, you said, 'Go tell John what you hear and see. The blind receive sight, the lame walk, those who have leprosy are cleansed, the deaf hear, the dead are raised, and the good news is proclaimed to the poor.' We knew that you meant you were the Messiah."

He looked at Jesus, eyes shining. "The first thing you said was you were healing the blind. You told the two blind men in Capernaum that it would be done for them according to their faith, and you healed them."

He grinned. "It seemed like a pretty good strategy to me. I was convinced you were the Son of David, the Messiah. If they were healed, why would I not be? So, when I learned that you were coming to Jericho, I was determined to find you. I heard you passing by and did just what they did. And you healed me too.

"The rest of that day was eye-opening." He chuckled. "The bright sun, the colors, watching everyone and everything move around me, connecting sounds and smells with what produced them, matching voices I'd heard my whole life with faces of people—it was all overwhelming."

Bartimaeus continued, "I wanted to go everywhere you went, hear and see everything. After being blind all my life, a new world had emerged for me. Yet, I sensed that even these amazing changes were small compared to what following you might mean.

"I walked with the crowd from ancient Jericho to Roman Jericho. You called out to the man in the tree, and when he spoke, I recognized his voice as that of the tax collector. We were all shocked when you went to eat with him instead of with the religious leaders from the synagogue. We wondered what went on inside the house that night, but we weren't invited to enter.

"After you had been inside the house for a while, I decided to find my family and friends to celebrate. I'll never forget seeing my mother's beautiful smile for the first time, my father's happy brown eyes, my sister's long shiny black hair. My mother made all my favorite dishes. My father opened his best jar of wine, and we talked and laughed and told stories late into the night."

Jesus listened with sheer enjoyment to the man's story. One of his favorite parts of any miracle was seeing afterward how God changed people's lives.

"The next day when I opened my eyes, I remembered instantly the events of the day before. I would have wondered if it had been a dream, but I could see. As I ate breakfast, I suddenly realized that I'd lost my source of income. No one was going to give me coins anymore. This hadn't occurred to me before being healed, but now I wondered what job I could do. I couldn't read, and I had never learned a trade. Who would hire an ex-blind man?

"As I was worrying about this, I heard a knock at the door. I opened it to find the tax collector, Zacchaeus! What could he possibly want? Surely he wasn't going to ask me to start paying taxes after one day! I invited him to sit, nervous about what he would say.

"But Zacchaeus told me, 'I was even more nervous yesterday with Jesus than you are now with me. Why would Jesus come to my house? This man that seemed to know everything. He was probably coming to punish me, to make an example of me, maybe even to bar me forever from the synagogue.

"'Yet as the meal went on, Jesus was simply kind to me. I

gradually realized that he was not there to punish me. He wanted to share a meal with me. He accepted me! It was astounding—and liberating.

"'In a burst of gratitude, I stood up and promised that I would give half of my possessions to the poor, and if I had cheated anyone, I would follow the law and give them back four times as much.'

"And then Zacchaeus said to me, 'Bartimaeus, I heard Jesus had healed your blindness earlier that day. I wondered what job a former blind man could get. It seemed that Jesus would want me to help you.'"

Bartimaeus slowly shook his head in wonder at the memory. "Zacchaeus offered me a job that day. He owns the groves of fig trees on this side of Jericho, and he arranged for me to learn how to take care of them. And now I have a job, as well as a new friend."

Bartimaeus smiled gratefully at Jesus. "So, I guess you could say that Salvation came to both of us that day, and both of our lives changed forever."

Reflect

1. During the 40 days of Jesus on earth, who do you think he went to visit? How do you imagine those conversations?
2. In what ways might Jesus have healed you physically? Spiritually? Have you been used by Jesus to help heal someone else in these ways?

Learn

In Luke 9:42, when Jesus says to Bartimaeus, "Your faith has healed you," the Greek word for heal, *sozo,* can mean both healed and saved; in fact, it is translated much more often "saved" than "healed." (*Strong's Lexicon*, word #4982). Notice how often Jesus pays attention to both physical and spiritual healing. One can often be an indicator of the other or even lead to the other.

Vignette 22

A Fresh Start for Zacchaeus

Exodus 22:1; Ezekiel 34:1-16; Luke 3:7-18

After enjoying a leisurely lunch with Bartimaeus and his father Timaeus, Jesus left ancient Jericho to travel to the newer Roman site of Jericho, taking the same route he had used two weeks before. His arrival this time was unannounced and quiet. He chuckled as he walked under the same sycamore tree, remembering the unusual sight of an adult businessman perched on a limb overhead.

As he approached the door of Zacchaeus' house, through a window, he saw Zacchaeus seated at a table, working. Zacchaeus looked out the window, gave a shout of delight, disappeared from view, and threw open the door to welcome Jesus into his home.

Zacchaeus offered Jesus a refreshing drink, and they sat down to chat. Jesus studied Zacchaeus' face, noting a new happiness and calm, which had replaced the stern, tense look he had worn when they first met.

Jesus asked him, "Tell me, Zacchaeus, what did the other tax collectors say when they learned of your plan to give away half your money?"

Zacchaeus gave a rueful laugh. "Most of them thought I had gone crazy or that I was ill and desperately trying to do a good deed before I died. They didn't understand at all. The Pharisees and synagogue leaders were skeptical. I think they were still upset because you came to my house and not theirs."

Jesus responded, "Those men are false shepherds, like some leaders of Ezekiel's time. They ignore the sheep who depend on them. They criticize you for being greedy, and they think they are righteous. But they also profit from the people without taking care of them. Instead of seeking after lost sheep like you, they condemn the lost ones and leave them to die.

"When I said I came to seek and save the lost, they knew I was quoting Ezekiel. They were angry because my comments about that passage revealed three truths—that they are like the false shepherds, that you are a sheep loved by God, and that I am the Son of God, doing what my Father has done throughout history." Jesus sat quietly for a moment, saddened by how often leaders were blind to the truth and callous toward the heart of God.

Then he looked back at Zacchaeus with a calm hope in his eyes. "But I believe you're different from them. For now, they're confused by the changes they see in your life, but soon they'll begin to wonder why you have changed."

Zacchaeus listened, his eyes fixed on Jesus' face. He answered, "I've been wondering how people will see me now. I don't know whether I'll continue in this job. Most people hate me because of it. They assume I'm cheating them and that I'm working with the Romans. Many people avoid me. They don't welcome me to the synagogue or invite me for dinner." Jesus nodded, acknowledging the pain, rejection, and isolation Zacchaeus had long felt.

"Some days I think I should find a job where other people would like and respect me, but I also think I could do good in this position. What would an honest tax collector be like?" He chuckled.

"When John the Baptist was teaching and baptizing out in the desert near the Jordan, some of the other tax collectors and I went out to listen to him. We thought he would incite the people to rebel. Instead, he told people to show the fruits of repentance. We were amused when he rebuked the leaders, called them a brood of vipers, and threatened them with judgment. They had often criticized us publicly, and we thought it was only fair that someone should do the same to them.

"Then some of my tax collector friends waded into the river to be baptized by John. They asked him what they should do, and he told them not to collect any more than they were required to do. And then John looked over at me. He knew who I was. I had seen him in Jericho."

Zacchaeus paused, recalling the moment. "I was uncomfortable. I didn't consider myself to be dishonest, but I had done some questionable things. I returned to my house that day, troubled.

"If I stay in this job and do it honestly, my friends might notice the change. When they ask me, I can tell them what you did for me."

Jesus gave him an approving smile. "That would show the fruits of repentance that John mentioned."

Then Jesus challenged him. "When Joshua arrived at this city a long time ago, my Father promised to give it to him, but that the city must be 'dedicated to God.' At that time, it meant the city would be destroyed, except for Rahab's family being saved.

"Many centuries later, your family has been saved. And now, through you and your testimony, salvation instead of destruction can come to this entire city"

Reflect

1. Who are the "tax collectors" in our society, or our particular communities, at this time?
2. Do we treat them as Jesus would, or mainly isolate and condemn them? What actions could we take with them that would please Jesus?

Learn

In Luke 19:10, Jesus quotes Ezekiel 34:16 to Zacchaeus. This is an example of a Jewish form of teaching called a *remez,* a clue or hint that reminds you of the larger context of a passage or situation. When Jesus used this technique here, he assumed his audience knew the context of the quote, and they would catch the three truths he was implying, and they would likely be angry. This is one good reason, whenever Jesus quotes the Old Testament, to check the original context for other meanings that might be connected to the New Testament context as well. I'm indebted to Ray Vander Laan for his explanation about *remez*.

https://www.thattheworldmayknow.com/remez

Vignette 23

A Changed Woman, a Changed Village

John 4:1-26; 1 Peter 2:4-9; Ephesians 2:21-22

The next morning, Jesus moved quickly in the Spirit to the village of Sychar, arriving just before noon. Going to a small house near Jacob's well, he knocked on the door, calling out, "Rachel! I need some water."

The door swung open. As Rachel saw Jesus, her face lit up with joy and surprise, and she threw herself into his arms. "The whole village heard about you dying. We *mourned* for you. But then rumors started about you coming back to life. We didn't know what to believe. I'm so glad the rumors were true."

She led Jesus inside and seated him at the table. She smiled as she gave him a cup of water, recalling that first conversation about water at the well. Rachel's husband, Levi, came from another room in the house and warmly greeted Jesus.

Rachel said, "Please rest. I'm going to invite my friends. They'll be so happy to see you again."

Jesus responded, "I'm looking forward to catching up with Levi. We'll see you in a while."

Rachel ran out of the house, stopping to knock at nearby homes, calling out the good news to people in the street. The news electrified the village; since that day almost three years ago, most of the village had come to believe in Jesus as the Messiah. Just like Rachel's, their lives had been transformed. Many had made the journey up to Galilee to hear Jesus speak, and several had been healed. They had returned to Sychar eager to share about the amazing teacher who treated them as children loved by God—despite their being Samaritans.

The people poured out of their houses, bringing food to Rachel's home and greeting him happily. As they ate together, he asked them about their lives during recent months, listening intently, encouraging them, bantering with them, and smiling. Then he spoke to them about their new lives in the Kingdom of God, challenging them to go to other towns and villages to share the good news.

After several hours, the neighbors left. Jesus looked at Rachel. "Would you like to take a walk with me?" She accepted gladly and set out with Jesus on the road leading west and south toward Mount Gerizim, about a mile and a half away. As they walked along, they talked about all that had happened to them since that first meeting by the well.

Shortly after Jesus had left, Rachel and Levi had made a lifelong commitment to each other and were married in a joyous celebration in the village. Rachel had tasted the living water and the sweetness of sharing that water. She had met the long-promised Messiah and learned to imitate his kind heart in her relationships with others.

She had begun a ministry to women who were single for various reasons. She shared her testimony with women who were widowed or divorced and with mothers who had been abandoned by their partners before marriage. She gave them hope and unconditional love, the same gifts she had received from Jesus. Many of those women had been at her house today.

Reaching Mount Gerizim, they climbed toward the summit, and sat near the spot where the Samaritan Temple had been built almost five hundred years earlier by Sanballat, during the time of Ezra and Nehemiah. For a few moments, they enjoyed the sunlight, the view of Sychar to the northeast, and the larger town of Shechem to the northwest.

"Do you remember what you said to me about this place?" asked Jesus.

"Yes," answered Rachel. "I told you our ancestors worshiped on this mountain but that the Jews worship in Jerusalem."

Jesus said, "My Father has often lived among his people in the Tabernacle or the Temple. People like having a physical place to visit, to be in God's presence, to worship together. There's a certain comfort in the rituals of sacrifice and ceremonies of worship."

"Yet the Temple of your ancestors here was destroyed about one hundred fifty years ago. And two weeks ago," Jesus said, "I told my disciples that the Temple of the Jews in Jerusalem will also soon be destroyed."

Rachel gasped. "When?"

Jesus replied, "The exact time is not important, but at that time, there will no longer be any Temple of the Lord left in the land. People will have no place to go worship or offer sacrifices. Much of their physical worship will be snatched from them.

"This is why I told you that true worshipers will worship in spirit and in truth. Soon, in the Jerusalem Temple, my Father will begin a new era in which he will live in every believer. Even after that Temple is destroyed, the Spirit in them will help them offer true and spiritual worship, no matter where they are.

"The place of worship will not matter, nor how many people are present. No animals or priests or buildings will be needed. I have given the perfect sacrifice once, for all. Every believer will be a priest, and I will build them into a spiritual Temple that cannot be invaded or destroyed."

Rachel pondered what Jesus had said to her. It transformed her perception of what it meant to be part of God's people. So long an outcast, along with the other Samaritans, she was now a welcome member of a worldwide, everlasting family.

Jesus said, "We can now worship my Father everywhere—here on this mountain, in Jerusalem—or anywhere else."

They bowed their heads, and Jesus prayed, "Father, we praise you for this privilege of being your children, of being able to come into your presence anywhere we are. We thank you for the renewal you have brought about in Rachel and Levi and for the many women who have seen your love through her.

"I ask you to build a spiritual Temple in this place, bringing together every person who has chosen to believe in you. Use Rachel and Levi as your servants in this town. For those who will soon believe in all of Samaria, we pray that you will be preparing their hearts to hear the kingdom message from your servants and that you will glorify your name in this place through them."

Jesus looked at Rachel. "Within the next year, a man will come from Jerusalem to bring the good news of the kingdom to all of Samaria. I need you and Levi to welcome him and share in his ministry. I want you to continue giving living water, this time to everyone. Will you do this?"

"Gladly," she answered. "It would be an honor for Levi and me." After rising from the ground, they retraced their steps to her house.

Reflect

1. When the coronavirus epidemic suspended church attendance and ministries or closed churches altogether, perhaps it was in some ways similar to the Temple being destroyed and the Jews losing their place of sacrifice and

worship. What do you think remained of Christian life during the pandemic when so many activities ceased?
2. Is it possible to fully live the Christian faith while isolated from other Christians?

Learn

Leen Ritmeyer has an informative article on the Samaritan temple on Mount Gerizim that helps us understand not only John 4, but also the enmity between Sanballat and Nehemiah in Nehemiah chapters 4 and 6.

https://www.ritmeyer.com/2021/01/21/the-jerusalem-temple-on-mount-gerizim/

Vignette 24

The Grateful Leper

Luke 17:11-19; Leviticus 13; Romans 12:21

Wednesday morning, Jesus journeyed to a small town on the border between Samaria and Galilee. About a mile out of town, he paused near a group of small, dilapidated houses. Just then, a man emerged from one of the dwellings and saw Jesus. His face broke into a broad smile, and he ran to greet Jesus.

"Nathan!" cried Jesus. "How are you? What are you still doing here? I thought you would go back to live with your family in Sebaste."

"I planned to," the man responded. "After you healed me and the other lepers, I was the only one who came back to this village. The others left. Some for Galilee, others for Judea. But with so many people here still suffering from leprosy, I couldn't leave without helping them.

"For the last month, I've been living here but working in a village nearby. With what I earn, I can provide a little food and medicine for those suffering the most, especially the children and elderly.

"The strange thing is that even though I'm around them every day, I haven't gotten sick. It's as if you not only healed me but also protected me from disease."

Jesus laid a hand on Nathan's shoulder, "Blessed are you, Nathan. You're the only one I healed who came back to thank me. You've shown my Father's heart to this village." Then Jesus probed, "But you've shared more than just food and medicine with these people, haven't you?"

Nathan nodded. "Everyone was shocked when I returned to the village, healed. They demanded to know what had happened, so I told them, and that made them even more eager to learn. Every night we gathered by the fire near our little houses, and I told them stories I had learned about you while working in the other village."

Nathan beamed. "They'll be so excited to see you! Could you stay a few minutes to meet them, please?"

"I'd be happy to," declared Jesus. They walked toward the houses, with Nathan calling out, "Everyone, come outside. Jesus is here. He's the one I've been telling you about!"

The doors of the hovels opened quickly, and people peered out at Jesus. They wanted to come to him, but ingrained warnings about staying away from clean people made them hesitate.

Jesus examined them, deeply touched by their suffering. He noticed a little boy with no ears or nose on his face and an old woman with only two fingers on one hand and one on the other. Most of them were covered with sores of different kinds. Their physical pain was horrible, but the emotional scars from years of rejection were even worse.

Jesus sat on a small bench near one of the houses. He smiled at the little boy. "Come here," he said quietly, reaching out a hand to the boy. The boy hung back a moment, but then a tiny smile appeared on his face, and he walked straight to Jesus.

Jesus took him in his arms and hugged him gently. He took the boy's head in his hands, placing them where his ears used to be. He smiled at him, then softly kissed his forehead in blessing.

The boy's mother stood nearby, spellbound. As Jesus removed his hands from her son, she gasped. The boy's head was completely healed—two perfect ears and a perfect nose. The boy reached up and felt his ears, then put his fingers on his nose. Then he giggled and ran to his mother. "Mom, I got my nose and ears back!"

The people crowded around to see for themselves, exclaiming in joy and surprise when they realized that not only was the boy's head healed, but all of him. Then, as if someone had given a signal, they all turned to look at Jesus.

Jesus reveled in the happiness of the boy and his mother. He saw a question forming on their faces. "If this man could heal the boy, could it be that he might ...?"

Jesus said compassionately, "Yes. You've suffered too long. Come." And one by one, he touched them, smiled at them, hugged them, and healed them all.

Overwhelmed with joy and gratitude, they invited him to share a simple lunch. As they ate, Jesus said to them, "Do you understand what happened today and with Nathan and the others before? Before, the law said that if anyone unclean touched a clean person, then that person also became unclean.

"My Father has sent me to purify and cleanse everyone. Your leprosy did not pass to me, rather, my purity passed to you and healed you.

"Just as now you are healed physically, my Father offers you spiritual purity and healing also. Before, sins could dominate and destroy you, and often, the sin was more powerful than the good around it. But now, the good has overcome the evil. My Father has made it possible for all sins to be forgiven and forgotten.

"I'm giving all of you a new mission. As you go back to your families and towns, tell everyone what the Lord has done for you. They may find it hard to believe. They may be worried about taking you back in, for fear that you are not fully healed, but you *are* healed. And you will never have this terrible disease again. When you look at yourselves in the future, remember always that what my Father has done on the outside, he is also doing on the inside."

Reflect

1. Who are the people who have been shunned and cast out in our society or communities?
2. Do you have any connections with any of these groups? What is the kindest way we can invite or integrate these groups into our communities or churches?

Learn

Read Leviticus 13 and Numbers 5:1-4 to see some of the rules concerning impurity and different kinds of diseases and how they not only impacted physical health but also how a person could be shut out of the community.

Vignette 25

Two Trips to Heaven, Two Resurrections

Luke 7:11-17; 8:51-56; 16:22; Exodus 15

After lunch, Jesus traveled in the Spirit to the edge of the village of Nain, where he strolled down the street to a cozy house and knocked on the door.

A young teenager opened it and welcomed Jesus with a cheerful smile. "Jesus, I knew you'd come today," proclaimed the young man.

Jesus smiled. "How did you know that, Josiah?"

"Because sometimes when I dream, I see some things that are happening in heaven. Or I see what's happening on earth, as if I'm in heaven. It's like I'm still connected from my time there. In my dream, I saw you walking down the road to our house, and now you're here."

Josiah's mother, Anna, heard their voices and came to greet Jesus. "I'm so glad to see you back. Josiah told me his dream, but I didn't know if you were even near here."

Jesus hugged her, then the three of them sat. Jesus said, "The last time I was in this house was after I met you on the road near the cemetery."

"The most amazing day ever!" Anna exclaimed. "I thought my life was over, after losing my husband, then Josiah. And in two minutes on the road, you changed everything. We were all stunned. When we got back home, we invited everyone in the village to a party, and it lasted till late that night."

Jesus asked Anna, "Could I stay with you this afternoon? I would love to see how both of you have been since that visit."

"Of course. Please eat dinner with us," responded Anna. "You know you're always welcome here."

Just then another knock came at the front door. Josiah jumped up to answer it and swung the door open. "Rebecca!" he exclaimed, ushering a young girl about his age and her parents into the living room—Jairus, the synagogue ruler from Capernaum, and his wife Fulvia.

When they saw Jesus, they came straight to him. Fulvia beamed. "Yesterday Rebecca said she dreamed you'd be here today. We heard that you had risen from the dead, but we didn't know what to believe. We tried to persuade her that maybe the rumor wasn't true and not to get her hopes up. Even if you were alive, how could she know you'd be here, of all places?"

Jairus patted his daughter on the shoulder. "But she insisted, and I'm so glad we came.

Jesus rose and hugged them all. "I'm glad you did, too, Jairus," he said. "Rebecca, it's so good to see you well." She smiled shyly at him, then Josiah tugged on her sleeve, "Let's go see my friends." They scurried out of the house while Jesus and the three parents settled down to catch up.

Jesus said, "I'd like to hear about your lives since your children came back to life."

Anna began, "I see everything now in terms of before or after. Before you raised Josiah, things were grim, uncertain, desperate. I felt no one really cared about me. When Josiah died, I honestly thought my life would soon be over as well. I didn't want to live anymore.

"After you raised Josiah, things got better for us. One of the businessmen in town gave me a job, and now families invite us to eat dinner with them sometimes. I know it's because they just want to know more about how it all happened, but now Josiah and I have more friends and feel hopeful about the future. They want to know more about you, too, so I'm happy to tell them the story and that I believe you're the Messiah.

"My friends asked me why I thought you had helped me and not the more important people in town, who had lost children. I felt terrible for them, but I had no answer. I only knew that when you raised Josiah, you showed me you cared about me."

Jesus nodded. "Some don't understand it. Others don't believe it, and some are envious or even angry when others are resurrected and their loved ones are not. It's natural to feel that way and to wonder what it would be like to come back to life."

Fulvia confessed, "Before you raised Rebecca, God seemed distant, unresponsive, even capricious. I remember that as Rebecca got sicker, I kept praying that God would heal her, but it didn't seem like God heard me. In desperation, I sent Jairus to find you, Jesus, hoping you could help us. But she died."

Fulvia voice caught on those words, and she bowed her head a moment. She continued, "I was heartbroken, and I admit I was angry with God for not answering me. Then Jairus came in with you and whispered in my ear, 'Jesus said not to be afraid, only believe, and she would be healed.'

"I had no words to answer him. I wanted to believe it, but I thought that healing was for sick people, not dead ones. And then she was standing up, alive, and we couldn't stop hugging her."

All four of them wiped happy tears from their eyes. Jesus told them, "My Father also knows the sorrow of losing a child and the joy of receiving him back alive again."

Fulvia declared, "Now I believe God does care about each one of us personally and that we matter to him. He seems a lot closer now, more responsive. I see his love more each day, in small and big things."

"He does care about each one of you infinitely." Jesus assured them. Finally, he turned to Jairus. "And you, Jairus? How are people reacting now in Capernaum?"

"People don't know what to believe yet," Jairus responded. "We all heard the news of your death. Some of the strict Pharisees and rabbis seemed to think Caiaphas and the Sanhedrin were right to sentence you, but you taught and healed so many here that most of us were just devastated and angry. Just a couple of days ago, the first reports trickled in about your resurrection. Since then, you've been pretty much the only topic of conversation in town."

Jesus answered them with a twinkle in his eye, "Josiah, Rebecca, Lazarus, and I are among the first members of a new family. And there are more. Have you heard about the saints who came out of their tombs the day I died?

"My Father is demonstrating what will happen eventually to all those who believe in him. Every one of them will be resurrected and live forever, including you three parents, of course. But while you wait for that moment, you're blessed to have children who have already experienced it and glimpsed heaven in the process. Take advantage of this gift."

The conversation continued, and the afternoon passed quickly. As evening drew near, Fulvia and Anna prepared a meal. Soon, Josiah and Rebecca returned to the house, and the six of them gathered around the table as one family.

After giving thanks for the food, Jesus said to the teenagers, "Your parents and I have been talking about you this afternoon. I told them they were fortunate to have children who have already been to my house." He smiled at them. "What do you two remember most about your time in heaven?"

The two pondered a moment, then Rebecca answered, "It seemed like I was falling asleep, drifting away from my parents. Then angels came and carried me to the gates of a bright city. Two young, healthy people were standing by the gate as we arrived. Suddenly, I realized they were my grandparents. Even though I'd never seen them as young people, I knew them.

"They took my hands, and we walked together through the gates down a street that looked like gold. People smiled and laughed. Two young boys played with a small brown puppy, and a group of young men and women clustered around an older woman to listen as she told them a story. The smell of meat and pies drifted out of the windows on the street. It was amazing. I felt that I was home where I belonged, and that I would never be afraid of anything again.

"A woman came up to me, smiling, with a tambourine in her hand. My grandparents said, 'Rebecca, we want you to meet Miriam, a famous singer here. We know you love music and singing. Would you like to learn a song from her?'

"She was Moses and Aaron's sister. My parents had told me the story of our people leaving Egypt, passing through the Red Sea, and being saved by God. Now she wanted to teach me the song they sang that day as they celebrated on the shore of the Red Sea."

Fulvia said proudly, "When she came back from heaven, she taught the song to us. Now we sing it at home and in the synagogue. It's a song straight from heaven, a living part of our people's history."

Jesus nodded. "As my Father and I watched that day, we celebrated with them. Would you sing it for us, Rebecca?"

Rebecca blushed shyly but agreed. As she began, Jesus and her parents joined in. Anna and Josiah were fascinated. They were hearing a song that had been created more than a thousand years before. Something that in the synagogue had always been just words on a page now came to life with a melody and rhythm.

When they finished, Jesus smiled at Josiah, "What about you, Josiah? What do you remember?"

Josiah answered, "Just like Rebecca, an angel carried me to a beautiful city. My father met me there. I was so little when he died that I hardly remembered him, but I knew who he was.

"As we toured the city, he showed me buildings, the parks, and a river flowing through the center with fruit trees on both sides. My father introduced me to his friends and to others he had met in heaven.

"He told me stories about Nain—the moment when he and my mom found out she was pregnant, the day I was born, the first months of my life, playing with me and teaching me to walk, and those last few days when he was sick and died. He told me that the worst part was he didn't want to leave me or my mom. He would have done anything to stay." Tears welled up in Josiah's eyes.

"Eventually, we arrived at a certain home in the city, and my father knocked on the door. He said with a gleam in his eye, 'I've wanted you to meet this person. You don't know him, but you're connected to him.' I was wondering how that was possible when the door opened, and my father and he hugged each other like old friends. My father said, 'Josiah, I want you to meet the person I named you for—Josiah. You've studied our history; who could this be?'

Josiah's eyes sparkled. "It was King Josiah. My father had named me for him, because the Word says, 'Never before nor after Josiah was there a king like him who turned to the Lord as he did—with all his heart and with all his soul and with all his mind and with all his strength, in accordance with the Law of Moses.' My father wanted me to live that way too—and now I was meeting him.

"He told me stories—how he became king when he was eight years old, how he found the law, how they tried to obey everything that God wanted them to do. He encouraged me to follow God with all my heart too.

"When we left the house and were again walking through the city, I heard a voice from a distance, 'Young man, I say to you, get up!' I knew I had to obey the voice and leave the city.

"My father heard the voice, too, and he said, 'The master Jesus is calling you, and you must go.' But then he placed his hands on my shoulders and with a tear in his eye, he said, 'And when you go back,

After the Tomb

tell your mother I love her and I miss her. I can't wait to see her here one day.'

"When I came back, instead of being in my house, I was lying on a stretcher in the middle of a road. A man stood by the stretcher, smiling down at me. People from the village crowded around, staring with amazement. Then the man repeated, 'Get up.' I got up and heard a gasp behind me. I turned around to see my mother's face. She was shocked. She couldn't believe it…but she was *so* happy." Josiah grinned at his mom. "I'll never forget her face and how she wrapped me up in her arms and cried."

Anna was weeping again, but with tears of gladness, remembering that amazing moment, and the reminder of her husband's love and concern for her.

Jesus said to them all, "You are blessed. Though you've passed through grief that many families do not, you've also received blessings they have not. Because Josiah and Rebecca have been to heaven and returned, you know for certain what's waiting for you when you die. Your neighbors, your friends, the people in town all know about what your families have been through. Continue to be my witnesses to everyone, not only in Nain but other towns in Galilee."

Reflect

1. What would it be like to have someone in your family who had died, gone to heaven, then come back to live in your house? (perhaps like the book or movie "Heaven is Real!"). What would you ask them? How would that change your attitude about heaven?

2. How much do you think about heaven? How could thinking about heaven help you live better on earth?

Learn

I highly recommend Bodie Thoene's A.D. Chronicles series. The seventh book, *Seventh Day,* tells the story of the widow of Nain and her son and the story of Jairus' daughter. One fascinating scene shows the two families together for supper, and suddenly, the parents notice that their children are singing a song the parents don't know. They ask the children what the song is, and the children respond that it's one they learned while in heaven briefly.

VIGNETTE 26

CONFESSIONS AT BREAKFAST

John 21; Luke 5:1-11; Mark 14:51-52

The disciples arrived from Jerusalem late Thursday afternoon, about 12 days after the angel had sent them to Galilee. Seven of them had gone out to fish on the Sea of Galilee to provide food for the group of travelers. It had been an exhausting trip, followed by a long night. To make things worse, they had no catch to show for all their work. Their favorite fishing spot, about a hundred yards from the warm springs on the western shore south of Capernaum, had not yielded even one fish.

As the sky lightened in the east, they glumly hauled in the nets one last time before heading to shore and a much-needed rest. Just then, movement on the shore caught Andrew's attention. In the darkness before the dawn, he thought it was a person, but he couldn't make out who it was.

A man called out to them, "Friends, did you catch any fish?" His tone was slightly humorous. The tired fishermen answered him shortly, a slight edge in their voices, "No."

The man persisted, "Why don't you try throwing your net on the right side of the boat?" Again, the light tone, which only irritated them. But to satisfy the man, or perhaps to prove him wrong, they cast the net once more.

The net disappeared sharply under the surface and the boat tilted heavily to the right. The water frothed all around them, bubbles rising from below. The men quickly grabbed the edges of the net and began to haul it in, but they couldn't get it all in the boat. Shouting to one another, they turned the boat and started towing the net toward shore.

"It must be a huge catch!" marveled James, looking over at John. Oddly, John wasn't even looking at the net or the water. He stared intently at the man on the shore. Then John turned to Peter and said quietly but urgently, "Peter, it's the Lord."

Peter glanced at John, then at the man onshore. Suddenly it all fell into place. This had happened before. That time, he had begged the Lord to go away from him. This time, he couldn't wait one more second to be with him.

Throwing on his cloak, he jumped into the water. Throughout the long journey from Jerusalem, he had wondered when he would see Jesus again and what he would say to him. His eagerness drove him through the water. Finally, he staggered onto the shore and into the outstretched arms of Jesus. "Welcome, Peter," he said. Then they watched the boat slowly grind onto the rocky beach.

Stumbling off the boat, the disciples sat wearily on rocks around the fire. Knowing how tired and hungry they were, Jesus had prepared breakfast for them. He told Peter, "Bring some of the fish you just caught."

Peter waded into the water and selected several fish from the thrashing pile, marveling that the net hadn't even torn.

"And so we meet again in Galilee," remarked Jesus. Giving thanks to his Father, he passed the food to them, and they accepted it with a touch of wonder in their eyes. Were they really sharing a meal together with Jesus by the sea? They knew it was true, but some wondered if it was a dream from which they would awake, plunged back into a world where Jesus was still dead.

Hunger satisfied, Peter said to Jesus, "We were talking among ourselves on the way home from Jerusalem," adding with a rueful smile, "and this time, it wasn't about which of us were the greatest—far from it.

"We agreed that the next time we saw you, we would beg you to forgive us for abandoning you that night." Peter's lips quivered, and he looked down for a moment. "And my actions were even worse. I denied you three times. I know you've forgiven me, but it's haunted me every day since."

Thomas ventured, "For hours, we wondered what happened with you and Annas, Caiaphas, Pilate, and Herod. After we ran away from the garden into the city, we finally stopped and went to Caiaphas' neighborhood. We wanted to see what news we could hear from people going in and out."

Nathanael said, "We were afraid to get too close to Caiaphas' house. The soldiers had almost arrested us once that night. We followed the crowds from there to the Fortress where Pilate was, to Herod's Palace, and back to the Fortress. We saw you from a distance, but we didn't even have the courage to ask what was happening."

James added, "Suddenly the crowd gave a bloodthirsty roar and poured out of the Fortress courtyard, coming straight toward us. We panicked and ran like cowards back to the house."

Andrew said, "When John returned to the house on Saturday morning, he told us how they tortured and crucified you, how you suffered for hours on the cross. Everything you predicted weeks before had happened. Not only were we ignorant then, but we weren't even with you that night when you needed us the most."

James concluded, "We knew we should have stayed to help you somehow, but we just kept running." The others nodded, tears in their eyes, remorse plain on their faces.

Jesus slowly looked around the circle, locking eyes with each man, feeling their shame, seeing the unspoken questions in their minds. Would he ever trust them again? Would they be forgiven, but no longer part of his mission? The anxiety of the past several days weighed on them heavily as they waited for his response.

"You are all still my brothers and my disciples. I still love you," Jesus assured them. "You are precious to me." They breathed out as one, relieved—pardoned.

"Though it's true I felt alone when you left that night, I was glad when the soldiers let you go, as I asked them to do. My Father and I would need you after my resurrection. In this way, you were not arrested. Now you are ready to serve."

They looked at him earnestly, given new hope and purpose.

"But tell me," said Jesus with a grin, "after that night in the garden, did Mark ever get his clothes back?" Caught off guard, the others stared at him for a moment, then broke out laughing.

Becoming serious again, Jesus told them, "I'll tell you more about that night during the days to come—whether with all of you or in private." Several of them shifted uneasily at this. "But we have much to do in these few days together. I must tell you more about the new Kingdom of my Father, which is now also yours. You were not ready to hear this before, but now you will be my ambassadors, and you must learn what to say and do as you share the Kingdom.

"Come. You've had a long journey, and you must rest before the Sabbath. Gather the fish and follow me."

James put out the fire while others loaded the fish into baskets in the boat, counting as they went. "A new record," said Nathanael. "One hundred fifty-three fish should be enough to feed our group for several days."

Jesus took Peter to one side, away from the others. He looked at him searchingly and asked, "Peter, do you love me more than these?"

Peter was confused by the question. "Yes, Lord. You know that I love you."

Jesus nodded and said cryptically, "Feed my lambs."

Uncertain what to say, Peter remained silent.

Again, Jesus said, "Peter, do you love me?"

He answered, "Yes, Lord. You know that I love you."

Jesus replied, "Then take care of my sheep."

Nonplussed by the strange conversation, Peter still said nothing, trying to understand.

A third time, Jesus said to him, "Peter, do you *love* me?"

Still wondering what Jesus was really trying to ask, Peter replied in a wounded tone, "Lord, you know all things. You know that I love you."

And Jesus said again, "Feed my sheep."

Peter gave Jesus a quizzical look and a slight shrug of his shoulders.

Jesus continued, "When you were younger, you dressed yourself and went where you wanted, but when you are old, you will stretch out your hands, and someone else will dress you and lead you where you do not want to go."

What could Jesus mean? Questioning his love, yet restoring Peter, affirming that he was called to care for Jesus' followers, then speaking about the future. Was Jesus trying to tell him he might be arrested or how he might die? Peter was hopelessly bewildered.

Noting this, Jesus spoke more simply to convey the heart of his message. "Peter, no matter what else happens, follow me." And with that, Jesus affirmed that first call three years before, restoring Peter to his role among the disciples.

They stood together in companionable silence for a moment, watching the other disciples clean up. Peter saw John approaching. Wanting to see what Jesus might answer, Peter asked, "Lord, what about him?"

Jesus shook his head and only replied, "If I want him to remain alive until I return, what difference would that make to you? You must follow me."

Musing, Peter followed Jesus as he led the group away from the shore and toward the mountain to reunite with the other disciples.

Reflect

1. This is the third time the Bible records the disciples seeing Jesus after his resurrection. What questions would you have had for Jesus at breakfast that morning?
2. After a person has sinned and been forgiven, what actions or attitudes help him or her move forward and continue to grow, in spite of failing like Peter?

Learn

Bargil Pixner has excellent maps and information about the Sea of Galilee in the time of Jesus, in particular this section of the shore near Capernaum and Tabgha. Since Pixner lived in that area several years, the book has invaluable knowledge about the geographical background of Jesus' ministry in Galilee. Pixner, Bargil. *With Jesus through Galilee, according to the fifth Gospel*. Rosh Pina: Corazin Publishing, 1992.

Vignette 27

Day of Testimony

Psalm 146:7-9; Isaiah 35:5-10; Matthew 7:14; 11:12; Luke 14:28-33

By Saturday morning, word had quickly spread that Jesus was back in Capernaum, and the synagogue was packed well before the service began. Jesus and his disciples arrived amid a buzz of anticipation. Every eye followed them as Jairus showed them to the seats of honor.

Jairus decided to interrupt the synagogue's normal schedule of Torah reading for this unusual occasion. After the usual opening benedictions and the Shema, he invited Jesus, "Rabbi, Lord, please speak to us."

Jesus rose and asked for certain scrolls from the synagogue attendant. All the people stood in respect and anticipation of the reading of the Word.

Unrolling the first scroll, Jesus read, *"He upholds the cause of the oppressed and gives food to the hungry. The Lord sets prisoners free; the Lord gives sight to the blind; the Lord lifts up those who are bowed down; the Lord loves the righteous. The Lord watches over the foreigner and sustains the fatherless and the widow, but he frustrates the ways of the wicked."*[1]

The assembly nodded at the familiar psalm. Then Jesus took the second scroll and continued, *"Then will the eyes of the blind be opened and the ears of the deaf unstopped. Then will the lame leap like a deer, and the mute tongue shout for joy."*[2]

Jesus asked the attendant to hold the scroll, then motioned to the people to sit. His eyes moved slowly from those nearest him to those seated at the sides and upward to the women and children overflowing the balcony. The crowd became utterly still as they waited for Jesus to comment. Each person felt as though Jesus was looking past their faces into their very souls.

Jesus began, "During the last three years, you've seen each of these scriptures fulfilled before your eyes, or you've heard stories from your friends. Some of you believed and followed me." Many nodded as they recalled the amazing miracles.

"Others of you refused to accept signs that were more numerous and compelling than those seen in Sodom, Tyre, Sidon, and Nineveh." Some of the Pharisees and teachers of the law shifted in their seats and looked away from Jesus.

Jesus said softly, "I plead with you to open your hearts and believe. If you do not, you are in danger of worse punishment than the people of those towns." The crowd listened to this warning with bated breath, their eyes darting back and forth between Jesus and the sullen faces of the leaders. Jesus studied each of the men soberly, sad rather than angry.

He took a deep breath, smiled, and said, "Andrew, could you bring your friend to me, please?" The people murmured and craned their necks to see who was going forward.

Jesus knelt as Andrew led a young boy to him. Jesus grinned and hugged the child. With his arm still around the boy, Jesus prompted

---

1. Psalm 146:7-9 (NIV)
2. Isaiah 35:5 (NIV)

him, "Daniel, tell them what you gave me." Eyes large, slightly overwhelmed by the people, the boy exclaimed, "I gave you our *lunch*!" The people chuckled, as did Jesus.

Jesus said, "Some of you were there the day Daniel and his brothers and sisters gave me their five loaves and two fish. Because they did, they helped fulfill the Psalm that says my Father gives food to the hungry."

Jesus glanced at Daniel's mother, who was proud and yet blushing. As she smiled at Daniel and Jesus, she brushed a tear from her eye. Her children had fulfilled a Psalm. The thought was overwhelming. Jesus rose to his feet as Andrew took the boy back to his mother.

Jesus gestured to another woman sitting in the balcony. "Ruth! I'm glad you're with us again. What did my Father do for you?" Nervous, yet resolute, Ruth answered, "He healed me when I touched the hem of your garment, because I believed you were the Messiah."

Watching her, Jairus remembered that moment. He had been standing three feet from her when she was healed. At the time, he thought the delay caused by her healing had cost his daughter's life. It had not. Once again, he felt a rush of gratitude as he remembered receiving his daughter back from death.

"Your faith healed you," Jesus affirmed her. "The Lord lifted you up when you were bowed down."

Jesus' gaze went to the entrance of the synagogue. Just outside the door, looking in, he saw his friend, the Roman centurion, and his servant. "Our friend of great faith," Jesus proclaimed. "Marcus, how is your servant?"

The centurion placed a hand on the young man's shoulder. "Thanks to you, he is completely well and has never been sick again." The people marveled at the healthy young man. Marcus continued, "You are truly the Messiah. Theo and I will serve you however you wish as long as we live."

Jesus smiled at him. "And so the Lord watches over the foreigners as well—and loves them."

During the next few minutes, Jesus called on two blind men he had cured, a demon-possessed man who had also been mute, and the paralytic whose friends had brought him to Jesus. Each gave a short, heartfelt testimony to how Jesus had transformed their lives.

The room quieted as people reflected on the testimonies. Then everyone fixed their attention on Jesus, who said, "The law requires two or three witnesses for something to be established. You have just heard eight people testify to what my Father has done through me. During the past three years, you saw with your own eyes these messianic prophecies come to life and fruition. Many more could testify as well."

The people digested his words. Many were convicted, while others still looked uncertain. Jesus scrutinized their hearts. Then he took the Isaiah scroll from the attendant once again.

The people stood as Jesus read, *"Water will gush forth in the wilderness and streams in the desert ... And a highway will be there; it will be called the Way of Holiness; it will be for those who walk on that Way. The unclean will not journey on it; wicked fools will not go about on it. No lion will be there, nor any ravenous beast; they will not be found there. But only the redeemed will walk there, and those the* Lord *has rescued will return. They will enter Zion with singing; everlasting joy will crown their heads. Gladness and joy will overtake them, and sorrow and sighing will flee away."*[3]

The attendant returned the scroll to the Torah cabinet. Jesus sat in Moses' seat and explained, "I've told you about this Way for three years. It's the narrow way that leads to the kingdom of heaven. Yet it goes through the wilderness. It's full of blessings and joy, but it can also be dangerous. Violent people may attack and persecute you if you are part of my kingdom. But at the end of the Way, you will enter Zion with singing, gladness, and joy. And sorrow and sighing will flee away.

"I will be with you only a short time. My Father and I yearn for

---

3. Isaiah 35:6; 35:8-10 (NIV)

each of you to be part of our kingdom." His eyes pleaded with them. "It's for every one of you, without exception. During the days to come, weigh in your hearts what it would mean for you to follow me. It will cost you everything, but in return, you'll receive everything my Father and I have for you."

He raised his hands and called on his Father to bless each one, then dismissed them. Thoughtful and sober, they quietly filed out and went to their homes.

Reflect

1. What do you think prevented people in Capernaum, Bethsaida, Chorazin, and other places from believing and following Jesus? What else might be done to convince them?
2. If you gave your testimony as these eight people did, what story would you tell?

Learn

Study the background passages of these testimonies: boy with loaves and fishes, Jn. 6:8; a woman with the flow of blood Lu. 8:43ff; Roman centurion and servant, Lu. 7:1-10; two blind men, Mat. 9:27ff; demon-possessed and mute man, Matt. 9:32ff; paralytic, Lu. 5:15ff; two or more witnesses, Deut. 19:15.

Vignette 28

Supper at Matthew's House

Matthew 9:10-13; 17:27; 8:11; Acts 4:34-35; John 21:25

All the lamps were lit in Matthew's house that Sabbath afternoon. A young lady sat in the doorway and played a happy tune on her flute. Outside, children chased each other around the house, giggling and shouting to each other.

Inside, a startling mix of people conversed with animated faces and energetic gestures. Some of the women who had accompanied Jesus during his ministry in Galilee; one of Matthew's tax collector colleagues who learned about Jesus when Peter paid him with a coin that still smelled like a fish; Jael, a young woman who had first heard Jesus when he told the story of the prodigal son; the eleven disciples; Mary Magdalene; Jesus' mother Mary; Ruth, who had been healed by Jesus and testified that day in the synagogue; the centurion Marcus and his servant Theo, and others. It felt like a large, rambunctious family reunion.

Soon Matthew called everyone to eat. The adults gathered around the tables in the center of the room, while children sat in groups near the walls. Matthew said to them all, "Welcome to my home. You honor us with your presence. We're especially glad to have Jesus with us again."

With a smile, he continued, "It reminds me of the first time some of us ate here together. Not everyone was happy about it, but we're glad all of you are here." Raising his hands and looking toward heaven, Matthew gave thanks to God for each person, and for the blessing of sharing a meal together.

Peter's mother-in-law, Hannah, supervised those serving the food. While people settled around the tables, Jesus beckoned to a young woman. "Jael, come sit with me tonight."

Jael looked surprised and a little shy, but came and sat at Jesus' right.

As they ate, Jesus asked her quietly how she had been during the last few months. She answered him, but her words were halting and her manner rather uncertain. Laying his hand on her shoulder, Jesus asked kindly, "What's wrong, Jael? Tell me what you're thinking."

At first, her eyes remained on her plate, but then slowly, she looked up at his face. The understanding there compelled her to speak. "It's just that … you know who I am and what I've done. The Pharisees have asked you why you welcomed sinners and ate with them. They were looking at *me* when they said 'sinners.' They also know what I've done. They said I shouldn't even be allowed in the synagogue."

The sting of that rejection and the thought that it might be justified weighed on her. She gathered her courage and revealed the deepest longing of her heart. "Do I really belong here? Would you—or anyone—truly love me and forgive me?" Tears filled her eyes, and she looked down, cringing inside as she recalled how others had responded, with or without words.

Jesus tightened his grasp on her shoulder, and said softly to her, "Jael, look at me."

Reluctantly, she turned to him.

"Let me tell you a story that many people don't remember. Generations ago, one of my ancestors was a woman named Rahab. She was a prostitute and not an Israelite. Yet, when the Israelite spies came to survey the city of Jericho, it was Rahab who offered them hospitality and protection, saving their lives. In the battle that followed, she and her family were protected and became part of the Israelite nation.

"You're worried that you don't belong in this family, but you are an important part of it, just like Rahab." He waited until she met his eyes again. "Just as Rahab blessed her family and Israel, you'll do the same for your new family here."

She searched Jesus' kind eyes, seeing love and forgiveness. At that moment, she decided she would believe his words and live them. He nodded as he saw the newfound resolution in her eyes.

He smiled again at her and handed her a dish. "More bread?"

Laughter and joy filled the room. Jesus rose from the table, content as he watched faces animated by interest, love, and concern. "Such a varied group!" he mused. "After my Father brings people to heaven, the first supper there will be like this."

Jesus wound his way to a corner where a group of women had gathered. Several of them, including Salome and Susanna, had seen most of the events of his ministry. Two were widows. One woman had been "put away" by her former husband. Several had husbands with them who had also believed in Jesus and encouraged their wives to minister to Jesus and the apostles.

Jesus sat with them and scanned the faces of the group fondly. "Faithful friends," he said. "I have such good memories of you.

"Salome, how many times did we enjoy your cooking at night by the road when we had been with people all day, walking from place to place? You could make a meal out of nothing."

She blushed as she accepted his words, then said, "But so did you, at least twice."

"And Susanna, you had a special gift for encouraging everyone when they were down or exhausted or hurting. Your smile and your gentleness prevented Judas and Simon the Zealot from arguing many a time. Peacemakers like you will be called daughters of my Father."

"Dinah and Jonas, you were always so generous. I remember one week when our group had a special need. We prayed that my Father would provide. The next day, you both took me aside and gave me even more money than we needed. I knew that you had sold your field and given us the money, but you said nothing about it, not wanting anyone else to know. My Father saw what you did in secret, and he will reward you for it.

"And Mary," he looked with affection at the woman from Magdala. They both remembered again that first day he had met her, driving the demons away from her soul forever. The others in the group understood. They had heard the story, seen the dramatic change in Mary.

Susanna said to Jesus, "We were glad to help you. It was an honor just to be around you, to learn from you, to see the miracles."

Salome added, "What I always remember is how you were so kind to people. On the day you found out your cousin John had been killed, you just wanted to go away and be alone, but the people followed you all day. We knew you were mourning, but you healed so many, then gave them food to eat. I was amazed."

Jonas smiled. "One day, we had walked about twenty miles on ou way back to Capernaum. We were so tired. The next morning, you said we needed to walk on to Gamla to teach there, but no one really wanted to go. Simon the Zealot had a sore throat. He was using that to get out of the trip and stay home. But you went to him and said you were sorry he was feeling sick, and you put your hand on his throat and healed him. He couldn't decide if he was happy to be healed or sad that he had to walk six miles. We laughed about it for the first couple of miles, and you were smiling, too, Jesus, weren't you?"

Jesus laughed out loud. "I admit it. I did enjoy it, and I don't think anyone else tried that again."

Dinah said, "Another time, a Pharisee wanted to correct you while you were teaching. Yet you weren't angry with him, or rude. I thought you were too easy on him. So later, I told you how you should have handled him." She shook her head. "I can't believe I was trying to correct the Son of God."

The others laughed, and her story spurred other memories of time spent with Jesus on the road, in homes, at meals, in synagogues, on the mountain. Taken together, they were a patchwork quilt revealing the character of Jesus, a permanent testimony to the heart of his ministry. These were the stories that might never be written down but were engraved on their hearts and remembered for eternity, the foundation Jesus laid for the group of believers who would follow him.

Finally, there was a break in the conversation. Jesus said earnestly to them, "In your own way, each of you has had a part in my ministry, and that will continue in the days and months to come. Share these same stories with whomever you meet—here in Capernaum, Bethsaida, Gamla, Sepphoris, or any other place." He paused. "I even want you to cross the sea to the Decapolis to tell people there, as well as those in Samaria and Phoenicia."

They looked soberly at him. Most of them had never been to the last few places he mentioned, whether out of fear or ignorance, disapproval from families, or a mistaken belief that those people were not important to God. They realized that just as they had seen him teach and live God's message, now it would be their turn to talk about Jesus to these people—and *be* Jesus to them. It was a daunting challenge. They looked at each other, feeling the awesome weight settle on them.

Jesus read their faces and their hearts, then reassured them, "But remember that I will be with you always."

Reflect

1. What would it have been like to accompany Jesus on his normal daily routine? What are the small tasks people might have done for Jesus? What stories could they tell that are not in the Bible?
2. If Jesus had invited you to leave your job and follow him, would you have done so? To what activities or role is he calling you now? What will you do?

Learn

Capernaum was the home base of Jesus' ministry. Far from being a small, unimportant town, it served as one of the centers of Jewish training. Many important rabbis had lived or taught in Capernaum, and they provided a significant part of the oral tradition and teaching of the Jews that became part of the Mishnah and the Talmud (oral and written commentaries on the Law). See a good overview of Capernaum (videos, pictures, and text) at this site:

https://www.holylandsite.com/capernaum-overview

Vignette 29

A New Celebration

Genesis 1-2; Matthew 14:19; 26:29

On the first Sunday morning Jesus was back in Galilee, people from all over Capernaum gathered near Hannah's house. They settled comfortably on the grass under several large trees nearby. A natural hush fell over the group as they looked expectantly to Jesus.

"Hear, O Israel! The Lord our God, the Lord is one." They joined him in the Shema. "And you shall love the Lord your God with all your heart, and with all your soul, and with all your mind, and with all your strength." Jesus added, "And you shall love your neighbor as yourself."

He looked up to heaven. "Blessed are you, O Lord, King of the Universe, because you gave me this new family and included them in your mission. Blessed are You because You granted hope in times of despair and new beginnings when everything seemed to have ended."

He was silent, meditating. Sensing that something different was about to happen, the people barely moved, their eyes fixed on him. The birds chirped softly, and the breeze whispered gently through the leaves above them.

"Throughout our history, our Father has always provided new beginnings. In the beginning, he created the heavens and the earth. The seventh day, which was the first Sabbath of rest, completed the creation. The next day, the first day of the week, marked the beginning of his perfect shalom—but it was soon marred by Adam and Eve through their disobedience.

"My Father sent me here to minister and sacrifice myself on the cross. I was killed on Passover Friday and was laid in the tomb on that Sabbath, the seventh day of the week. On the first day of the week when my Father raised me to life and brought me out of the tomb, he opened the door to restoring his perfect shalom between him and all creation.

"As Adam and Eve enjoyed that first creation, so you also are living in the time of a new creation, a new covenant. My Father has chosen you all to share his shalom with the rest of the world.

"In the coming years, I want my followers to remember this on the first day of every week—my resurrection, the new covenant, and the mission of shalom. I now establish the first day of the week as a time when those who believe in me and follow me will come together. I want you to encourage each other, share your lives, learn more about me, and listen to the Spirit whom I will soon send to you.

Complete silence reigned. Their eyes shone, and wordlessly, they reached out to the people near them, grasping hands or shoulders. How fortunate were they to witness these things! The honor humbled them; the responsibility awed them.

Jesus turned to Hannah, Joanna, John, and Andrew. "Please bring what I asked you to prepare." They hurried to the house, reappearing almost immediately with baskets of loaves and several jars of wine, setting them down beside Jesus.

Jesus took a loaf of bread in his left hand and a jar of wine in his right, just as he had done so many times—at meals with his disciples, at the yearly feasts, with the crowds near the Sea.

So many memories wrapped up in this simple act—the Bread of Life from heaven breaking the bread that reminded them of his broken body, the Living Water who turned water to wine for his first sign, sharing the wine that represented his blood.

His gaze drifted around the circle of his earthly family and his new family of friends and companions. He said to his disciples, "Do you remember what I said to you just a few days ago at the Passover supper?"

Matthew answered, "That you would not drink of this fruit of the vine from now on until that day when you would drink it anew with us in your Father's Kingdom."

Jesus nodded, raising his cup to the group, "Welcome to the Kingdom!" He blessed his Father for the occasion, the people, the bread and wine, then passed the elements to them all. The enormity of the moment unified and sobered them.

Reflect

1. What do you think the first celebration of communion in the church was like?
2. Does the celebration change, depending on the cultural or geographical context?

Learn

Perhaps you have celebrated communion for many years in the church, or just a few. Perhaps you are new or have not participated at all. What should be the focus of the Lord's Supper? In light of that answer, consider these additional questions. If you had to write down the "unwritten rules" of observing communion, what would they be? Who takes part in it? How often? When? If in a city or country, the elements of communion (bread and fruit of the vine) are not available, what should you do?

Vignette 30

A Sober Delivery from Joseph of Arimathea

Romans 8:28; Isaiah 53:4-12; Genesis 50:20; 1 Corinthians 4:2

Joseph of Arimathea had arrived late the night before from Jerusalem and had taken part in the simple service. Jesus greeted him afterward. "Welcome, Joseph! I hoped you would make it. What news do you bring?"

Joseph responded, "Things are in quite an uproar! Caiaphas is trying to convince the Sanhedrin to arrest you, which is awkward, because that means he must admit you are alive again. Many people now know you were raised from the dead, and they believe in you more than ever. I think he will fail. Yet what could Caiaphas possibly do to you now, even if he arrested you?"

Jesus replied soberly, "I warned him. I pray his heart changes, but his pride and ambition are still too strong for him. They will be his downfall."

Joseph nodded his head in sorrowful agreement. Then he asked Jesus, "Could I have a few minutes alone with you and your disciples? I've brought something for you."

Jesus took his arm and led the way to Hannah's house, where she stood at the door. He asked, "Hannah, could we have a few minutes in your home with a small group?"

"Of course," she answered. She offered them places to sit and brought them a drink, then took her place at the edge of the group.

His voice grave, Joseph began, "I have something to give to you. I thought you should decide what should be done with it." Hearing his tone, the others leaned forward and gave him their full attention.

Joseph knelt, opening the pack he brought with him from Jerusalem. With sad reverence he brought several objects out and laid them on the floor in front of Jesus. The others craned their necks to see, then drew a sharp breath as they recognized the objects.

The three spikes from Jesus' cross.

Joseph again reached into the bag and took out the burial garments and the head covering from Jesus' tomb, placing them carefully beside the nails.

The disciples stared at them, transfixed. Memories of that awful day and night flooded in again. At first no one moved or spoke, then slowly, they raised their eyes from the floor and looked at Jesus' face.

Jesus' gaze was locked on the items responsible for ending his life so painfully. Though Joseph had done his best to clean them before he came, bloodstains still showed.

For a full minute, Jesus said nothing, then finally drew a deep breath. "I would not want to live that day again." His face was drawn and grim. "These nails and linens remind us of great pain and loss. It's tempting to be angry and desire revenge against those who provoked this suffering."

Several of the disciples had tears in their eyes. Peter tore his gaze away from the nails, unable to look at anyone else.

"Yet because my Father can use anything for good for those who love him, what I see now are the instruments used to complete his promise to pay for all sins. The nails caused much suffering, but the suffering brought salvation to the world. Caiaphas meant it for evil, but God used it for good. Remember the suffering, but then tell people the final result that my Father seeks through it. If you do this, the suffering will have achieved its purpose."

The disciples processed Jesus' words, trying to overcome their sadness and anger. Yet he had given them a new perspective—defeat turned to victory, an apparent ending converted to a startling new beginning.

Joseph was the first to speak. "Lord, I kept these things out of respect for you and to remember that day always. I didn't want the soldiers or Caiaphas to have them. What do you want to do with them?"

Jesus answered him. "They've fulfilled the first part of my Father's plan, yet there is one more purpose they can serve."

He turned to Hannah and the disciples. "Like the bread and the wine, these objects now are witnesses, highlighting my Father's faithfulness, his ability to turn evil to good, his power to bring about my resurrection and Satan's defeat, and ..." he paused, "our love for you and every other person in the world, in spite of their sins.

"But I warn you all—in the coming months and years, some will want to look only at the nails or the linen, forgetting what my Father and I did. They will try to profit from them or gain power through them to manipulate others. Don't be deceived or distracted. Remember to focus on the love and the plan that my Father and I have for you all."

Jesus placed the items in the bag and gave it to Hannah. "Will you keep these here?" Speechless, she nodded and accepted the awe-full gift.

Reflect

1. Can you articulate the fine line between a person using such objects to edify others or manipulate them?
2. What objects in your life hold special meaning—edifying, reminding, or teaching you?

Learn

Consider the Catholic doctrine of relics found in the Catholic Encyclopedia, regarding parts of the cross, parts of saint's bodies, etc. Part of their justification in using such things is based on certain physical objects in the Bible that seemed to hold special significance and impart special power—the ark of the covenant; Aaron's staff; a jar of manna; the 10 Commandments; Elisha's bones (2 Kings 13:20-21); bread and wine; a handkerchief (Acts 19:12); an apostle's shadow (Acts 5:15); etc. Again, when is something useful for instruction and edification, and when do manipulation and superstition begin?

VIGNETTE 31

TAMING THE SONS OF THUNDER

1 John 2:22, 3:2; Philippians 3:21; John 21:21-23; Revelation 1:9ff; Matthew 24:23-26

On Monday morning after breakfast, Jesus and John headed south on the Via Maris, which ran by Capernaum, enjoying the breeze and the vista of the beautiful lake spread out to their left in the morning sun. Soon, they arrived at a cave overlooking the road and the sea, one of Jesus' favorite places of solitude when he needed to escape from the ever-present demands of the crowds. It was here that Peter found him the morning after Jesus had healed Hannah. It was here Jesus had rested after feeding the multitudes. Jesus and John sat down at the mouth of the cave and soaked in the beauty surrounding them in companionable silence.

Presently, John asked, rather timidly, "Jesus, I know that the first night you appeared to us, you proved to us that your body was real. But ...we've also seen you do things that we can't do—appear in places when the doors were locked, disappear, move around more quickly than we can. How can you do these things?"

Jesus smiled at his young friend. "My body now is the same as yours, but also different. It's like the caterpillar. First, you see it crawl along, then it wraps itself up in a cocoon, and finally, it emerges as a butterfly. You know that the caterpillar, the cocoon, and the butterfly are connected in some way, yet they are surprisingly different—and how each one transforms into the next is a mystery.

"Right now, you and the others only know the life of the caterpillar. One day, you'll also be butterflies. Just as the caterpillar cannot imagine what it's like to fly, you struggle to understand this." The confusion was still on John's face. "Someday your bodies also will be transformed to be like my body. You'll be like me, and you'll see me as I am."

John pondered this for a moment, then said, "Peter told me he asked you what would happen to me later, and you said, 'If I want him to remain alive until I return, what is that to you?'"

Jesus pursed his lips. "And …?"

"The next day, I heard Philip, Andrew, and Joanna talking about it, and Philip said, 'I wonder if that means John won't die?' Then they saw me and were embarrassed and stopped talking.

"Lord, what did you mean? Am I going to live here forever?"

Jesus turned a quizzical eye on John. "Can you guess how I might answer you?"

John replied in a slightly disappointed voice, "That the times and dates are not for me to know, but only our Father in heaven?"

"True," said Jesus. "For most people, learning too much about their future would burden their lives rather than help.

"But I can tell you that you will have many years to teach people about me. My Father will send you to faraway places to witness and serve. You'll suffer some for my name but also experience great joy and satisfaction as you show others the importance of living in love.

"You'll have time to write down much of what I taught and demonstrate how to live. As a matter of fact, to write about some things, you'll go to … unexpected places and see wondrous sights, of which you've had a small taste before," Jesus said mysteriously.

"Afterward, what you write will greatly encourage my followers and help them remain faithful to me."

Suddenly, they heard a voice hailing them from a distance. John's brother, James, was approaching on the road from Capernaum. They waved at him and waited as he came up the hill. He sat down beside them, panting. "I thought I might find you here!"

Jesus looked fondly at two of his closest earthly friends. "The Sons of Thunder!" he said with a small grin. "You've come a long way since the first day I saw you on that dock and asked you to follow me." He gestured to the main dock of Capernaum, just 150 meters down the hill from them.

"It was an honor to be called by a man who was becoming known all over Galilee. We could learn from you, and," James said, shamefacedly, "we thought people would be impressed that two poor fishermen had places of honor close to you."

John sighed. "We were impetuous and brash—and our mother liked it too."

Jesus inclined his head briefly. "I know. I remember the day she came to ask for special privileges for you. The other disciples weren't too pleased with you that day!"

"For so long, we didn't understand what it meant to serve instead of being served," James said. "Even at the Passover supper that night, none of us wanted to wash everyone's feet. Surely someone else should do that! We were so ashamed when you did it for all of us."

Jesus explained, "I was willing to do that to help you learn an important lesson, along with the new commandment to love one another. And you have begun to love …" he looked at them, "instead of calling down fire on people when they don't do what you want them to do."

The two hung their heads, then glanced up at him and saw he wasn't angry. They pursed their lips, then a sheepish grin slowly grew on their faces.

"I'm embarrassed to think about that day," admitted John. "Our pride was offended that the Samaritans would reject us. Who did they think they were? But the real question was, who did *we* think we were—Elijah? Commanding fire from heaven? We forgot God sent fire that day on the sacrifice, not on the people!"

He said humbly to Jesus, "Thank you for being patient with us. We still have a lot to learn about that kind of love."

"You do. Nevertheless, I believe in you both," Jesus gently replied. "That's why I've spent these three years with you. It's why you have been privileged to see things that many longed to see but did not—raising Jairus' daughter, my Father clothing me in light, being alone with me in the garden that night. You learned about who I am and the powerful works I can do. You also learned how I had to suffer.

"You said that you're able to drink the cup that I drank—and you will drink it! You're not yet what I want you to be, but you've grown and changed. And my Father, who began this work in you, will finish it. You will be like me, have God's power like me, and will suffer for me."

Reflect

1. Why do you think Jesus utilized different circles of followers—his closest friends in Peter, James, and John; the 12 apostles; the 70 sent on a mission; the 120 at Pentecost?
2. Is this a model we should follow in discipling and training people in the church?

Learn

Historically and geographically, Galilee is enormously important. The Sea and the Jordan River are the primary fresh-water sources in Israel. The Via Maris has been a key highway for travel, commerce, and military control for thousands of years. It's not surprising that this area of Galilee was the focus of much of Jesus' earthly ministry. Jesus visited all the towns and villages preaching about the kingdom, such as Magdala, Gennesaret, Tiberias, and Gamla. In fact, the area between Capernaum, Chorazin, and Bethsaida is called "the evangelical triangle" by some, because almost 70 percent of Jesus' words or acts recorded in the gospels occurred in that triangle, measuring about three miles by three miles by three miles.

Vignette 32

Life in Cana After the Wedding

John 2:1-11; Matthew 5:44-46

On Tuesday afternoon, Jesus moved quickly in the Spirit to Cana, appearing outside the city. He approached one of the larger homes, near the town synagogue. As he drew near, one of the servants was carrying water from the well into the house. He glanced at Jesus, did a double-take, and the jar slipped out of his hands. "Jesus, is that you?" he exclaimed.

"Yes," responded Jesus with a smile.

Drawn by the commotion, a young woman came out of the front door and looked inquiringly at the servant, then caught sight of Jesus. Her eyes and mouth opened wide, and then she ran over and hugged Jesus.

"Adah! It's so good to see you again," said Jesus, smiling into her shining eyes. A curious little face peeped out from the door. "And who is this?"

Adah stretched out a hand and beckoned to the girl. "This is our daughter, Adina," she said proudly. "She just turned two this week. I wish you had been at that party too!"

A young man now emerged from the house to be greeted by Jesus. "Jonah! How are you, my friend?"

"Happy!" Jonah answered. "Ever since you came to our wedding, it seems our life has been full of blessings. We were able to build our rooms onto my parents' home here. I enjoy helping my father's wine business, and Adina is wonderful." He scooped her up. She gave him a gap-toothed grin and patted his cheeks with chubby hands.

"I'm glad for you," said Jesus sincerely. "It's what I hoped for that night as we celebrated with you and your friends."

Adah invited, "Jesus, would you join us for supper? We'd love to talk to you more."

Adina begged, "Pleeaasee!"

Jesus laughed. "How can I refuse that face?"

As evening fell, many people gathered around the tables and filled the rooms of the large home. Jesus sat at one table with Jonah and Adah on one side and little Adina on the other. Across from him were their good friends, Barnabas and Bekah, and by them, Jonah's parents, Elisha and Daniela. The two couples had been close for years.

As the dinner progressed, Jesus asked about life in Cana and listened intently as people told him what was happening. Adina crawled up in Jesus' lap and snuggled against him as he put an arm around her. The evening passed quickly as the guests enjoyed the food and wine, and the conversation flowed. Adina soon fell asleep in Jesus' arms.

Jesus asked, "I know that life here is hard under Herod Antipas. What are people thinking and doing in this part of Galilee?"

Barnabas answered, "We try to live peacefully with everyone here, but the Zealots are becoming more active. They don't respect Herod Antipas at all. They try to ambush Roman soldiers on the roads or attack people who they think are sympathetic to the Romans. I hear they're quietly building up the fortifications at Gamla and Jodfat."

His wife Bekah added, "We're worried that the Romans will lose patience with them, and then all of us in this area would suffer—in Nazareth, Cana, Jodfat, and even Sepphoris."

Elisha said, "Several weeks ago, the Romans caught two Zealots stealing supplies from a Roman outpost. The thieves were crucified on two crosses at the nearest crossroads as a lesson to everyone."

Jesus pondered for a moment and replied, "One of my disciples, Simon, has contacts among the Zealots. He told me about that just before we left for Jerusalem." He sighed. "We cannot overcome evil with evil but only with good. Those who are children of my Father must love their enemies and pray for them. We cannot love only those who love us."

The group looked at him soberly. They knew he was right, but it was hard to imagine loving the Romans, who had oppressed the Jews for the last ninety years. There was silence around the table as the difficult challenge sank in.

A servant came to the table to refill the wine cups and take away the dishes. Jesus picked up his cup, looked at it, and smiled. As the servant turned to leave, Jesus stopped him. "Peniel, I have a favor to ask of you."

Puzzled, the servant asked, "Lord?"

Jesus said to the guests, "There's a story which you think you know, but you lack one piece of it. Peniel—tell them what happened here three years ago at Jonah and Adah's wedding." The guests glanced at each other questioningly and waited expectantly for Peniel to begin.

"Everyone was so happy at the party, and the whole village was here to celebrate," Peniel began. "But as the party went on, I noticed that the wine had almost run out, since it was the seventh day of the feast. I asked the other servants if there were any more jars of wine, but no one could find any. It seemed they hadn't prepared enough.

"We didn't know what to do. At any moment the master of the banquet, Barnabas, might call for more wine for a toast, and we didn't have any." Peniel glanced at Barnabas, who looked surprised yet intrigued. "The family would be embarrassed, and their reputation would suffer—especially since the family had the job of providing wine for the village!

"Jesus' mother noticed that we were worried and asked what was wrong. Then she brought Jesus. He told us to fill up some stone water jars and take some to Barnabas. We didn't see how that would help—it would only reveal our problem sooner and more publicly!

"But we filled the jars with water anyway. Then we poured some into the serving flasks, and it turned into red wine as it came out of the jar! When Barnabas took a sip, he congratulated the family for saving the best wine till last. It was the finest wine anyone had tasted that year in our village!"

This news stunned the guests. They remembered the wedding and the feast, of course, but this was the first time they had heard the true story of what had happened. They gazed at Jesus in wonder.

He explained, "The wedding feasts that we celebrate here give hints of the feasts to come in my Father's Kingdom, in heaven. He'll provide abundantly, without limit. He'll give his children the very best. But until then, you must follow me here, no matter what happens with the Romans, with Herod, with anyone or anything else.

"Just as my relationship with many of you began at the wedding feast years ago, at this feast tonight, I call you into a new covenant—to be faithful to me and to all who follow me.

"When I provided the wine three years ago, it was a foreshadowing of two themes. First, just as branches that remain in the vine produce fruit, if you remain in me, you will produce the fruit that God desires in his people. Producing godly fruit requires a close relationship with my Father, which results in deeper understanding, stronger devotion, and faithful imitation. When you remain in me, I will share the blessings my Father wants to give each of you.

"Second, the water I used that night was taken from the stone jars used for the purification rites. Although throughout history you used water to purify yourselves before approaching God in the synagogue or the Temple, at services, or at feasts. Now you'll come close to God and be purified and forgiven through my blood, which this wine now symbolizes.

"The blessings you receive from me and the covenant sealed by my blood will lead you to heaven where we'll celebrate a wedding feast eternally."

Then Jesus looked over at Adah and Jonah, patted Adina on the back, and said, "I think this little one is ready for bed." As each one went home, they were filled not with bread alone but also the promises Jesus had given them.

Reflect

1. How is it possible not to respond to evil with evil and yet at the same time protect the innocent?
2. How do you reconcile the many accounts of the people of God going to war in the Old Testament and zero accounts of his people going to war in the New Testament?
3. Is there a difference between how a nation or government might respond to evil (war, force, etc.), and what an individual can or should do?

Learn

Doug Ponder has an excellent article about the Jewish background behind the story of the wedding at Cana.

https://tabletalkmagazine.com/posts/why-did-jesus-turn-water-into-wine/

VIGNETTE 33
RECKONING TIME FOR ANTIPAS

Luke 8:1-3; Mark 6:17-29; James 5:1-6; Isaiah 58:6-14; Deuteronomy 30:19

Wednesday morning, Jesus set off for a pleasant morning walk to Sepphoris, about five miles away. He remembered numerous mornings like this one, when, as a teenager, he and his father Joseph traveled the five miles from their home in Nazareth to the city of Sepphoris. Though Sepphoris had been burned by the Romans shortly after Jesus was born, Herod Antipas had been rebuilding it in luxurious Roman style, complete with a large amphitheater, bath houses, businesses, and expensive villas.

To do this, Antipas required many skilled builders. Antipas' foremen contracted many craftsmen, such as Joseph and Jesus, to work on several projects, including the amphitheater, a small synagogue, and the villa of Antipas, overlooking the city.

When Jesus arrived at that luxurious villa, the steward Chuza hailed him from the garden gate. "When did you get here? We didn't expect you to come."

Jesus answered drily, "I would imagine Herod is not expecting me either, but I have matters to discuss with him."

Chuza led Jesus into the villa to Antipas' chambers, which the ruler used for meetings and business in Galilee. Jesus stepped into the room and stopped near the door. Antipas sat at a small wooden desk by the window, reading a letter. He stood to receive his visitor, but when he saw Jesus, he collapsed back into the chair, staring wildly at him. Jesus sat squarely across from Antipas and studied him deliberately.

"I thought ... I had heard that you were alive again," Antipas stuttered. "Chuza told me you had come from Jerusalem last week, but it seemed impossible." His hands trembled as he fumbled with the papers on his desk. "What do you want?"

Jesus replied, "When we were last together at your Jerusalem palace, you were pleased to see me, hoping for a sign. But it was not my Father's will to provide one at that time." Jesus gestured to himself, spreading his arms with a faint smile. "But today I *am* the sign—raised from the dead by my Father. What will you do with this sign?"

The question hung in the air between them. Antipas opened his mouth, but no sound came out. He cast a furtive glance toward Chuza as if seeking help, but Chuza showed just the merest trace of a smile and remained silent. Antipas dropped his gaze to the floor, then finally raised his eyes back to Jesus.

Jesus gestured toward the window; the elegant city of Sepphoris stretched out below on the beautiful hillside, basking in the morning sun. "Did you know that the first time I came to Sepphoris was when your foreman hired my father and me to help build this city?

"One day, when I was fourteen, we finished our work shift. We were walking through the heart of town toward my grandparents' house. Suddenly, a group of soldiers on horses charged down the street toward us, clearing a path for your chariot. We scrambled to the side of the road, and you passed by, not even looking at the people you had almost run down. I had heard others talking about you before, but that was the first time I had seen you. I thought you were so cold, so indifferent. My father had his arm wrapped around me, and his face was stern and angry."

Jesus studied the tetrarch's face. "Do you know why he felt that way about you, Antipas? Because when your father Herod slaughtered all the innocent babies in Bethlehem, shortly before he died, I was the baby Herod was trying to kill! However, an angel had warned my parents, and we escaped just in time. But many other parents in Bethlehem grieved that night. They didn't understand why their children were killed. It scarred them forever.

"My Father mourned with the parents of Bethlehem, and he was furious with Herod. What kind of punishment do you think my Father has prepared for your father for this crime and all the other murders he committed?

"And you followed your father's example of murdering innocents when you killed the prophet John, didn't you? Did you know John was my cousin?"

Antipas blanched.

"Why were you offended by John? Because he told you the truth, as a true prophet should, about your adultery with your brother's wife, Herodias!" Jesus' eyes flashed as he delivered this accusation.

"But Herodias was angry with John, so even though you knew John was a righteous and holy man, you let her goad you into killing him as the entertainment at your birthday party. You were weak, as well as evil."

Antipas' face paled even further, and he began to tremble.

Jesus continued, relentlessly, "You've oppressed the poor and the weak, the widows and orphans. You've lived in luxury while many starved. You've spent money on yourself, your palaces, and your pleasures when you should have cared for the people under your rule.

"You also allied yourself with the Romans to protect your power, no matter what it cost. Less than three weeks ago, thinking you could rid yourself of a threat and solidify your position once and for all, you helped Pilate sentence me to death."

A deathly silence gripped the room as Jesus surveyed Antipas grimly. Chuza was frozen to the floor, spellbound. No one had ever given such a tongue-lashing to Antipas. If they had, they would have been dead in less than a day. Yet, Jesus clearly possessed all power and authority here. Antipas cringed, desperate to escape, unable to meet Jesus' eyes.

Jesus lowered his voice. "What kind of punishment do you think is waiting for you, Antipas?"

Antipas shivered and panted in dread.

"Where is the prophet John, whom you killed? I tell you, he is alive again in Paradise, where my Father honors him for his faithful service.

"As for me—you and your soldiers mocked me just three weeks ago in your palace. You thought you had sent me to my death. But you see that I'm no longer dead. I'm alive—alive forever, and invincible.

"And *you* now stand liable in judgment before me and my Father."

Antipas collapsed. For several minutes the only sounds in the room were his sobs and cries.

Finally, Jesus said calmly, "Antipas, listen to me."

Slowly his crying ceased, and he raised his tear-stained face to Jesus, resigned to condemnation and punishment.

Jesus leaned forward, his eyes level with Antipas' face. "My Father and I desire mercy, not sacrifice."

Still sunk in fear and guilt, Antipas stared uncomprehendingly at Jesus.

Jesus continued, "My death on the cross was not what you and Pilate planned. Rather, it was a sacrifice that brought mercy. Through it, my Father offers grace to all who have sinned, no matter what the sin."

Antipas still stared. "This includes your sins that I just

mentioned, and your father's, and Pilate's, and everyone's. My Father may yet be gracious to you."

Antipas began to comprehend the words—but surely they couldn't be true? Was Jesus just giving him false hope before punishing him?

Seeing what Antipas thought, Jesus asked, "Do you remember what the prophet Isaiah said? His words are for you:

'Is this not the kind of fasting I have chosen, to loose the chains of injustice, to set the oppressed free, to share food and shelter with the hungry, to clothe the naked, to call the Sabbath a delight and honor it? If you do these things, your light will rise in the darkness, and the Lord will guide you always and satisfy your needs, and you will find your joy in the Lord.'"[1]

Antipas gradually calmed. Impossibly, he glimpsed some small hope where before was only grim judgment.

Jesus took a deep breath and stood, gazing down at Antipas. "There's still time for you to repent, for your sins to be wiped out, and for my Father to send times of refreshing to you. I set before you today life and death; I urge you to choose life."

Jesus departed the room with Chuza, quietly closing the door, leaving Antipas to wrestle with his decision.

Reflect

1. This book paints possible scenes of Jesus visiting Caiaphas, Pilate, and Antipas, and offering accusations

---

1. Isaiah 58:6-11 (paraphrased)

followed by mercy. What in the ministry of Jesus would support these possible actions?
2. How do we deal with political leaders who have wronged us or others, or with whom we strongly disagree?

Learn

The Bible mentions six Herods. The first is Herod the Great, who built numerous amazing projects such as the remodeled Jerusalem Temple, palaces at Herodium, Caesarea Maritime, Jericho, Masada, and more. He also was a bloodthirsty, paranoid tyrant who killed thousands of people, including the baby boys of Bethlehem (Matt. 2:1-12). This Herod had three sons mentioned in the Bible. One was Archelaus, who reigned over Judah when Jesus and his family returned from Egypt (Matt. 2:22); a second was Philip, tetrarch over Gaulinitis, including Caesarea Philippi (Luke 3:1, Matt. 14:3); a third was Antipas, tetrarch of Galilee who killed John the Baptist, as well as being part of Jesus' trial. Then Herod Agrippa I, a nephew of Antipas, was the man who killed the apostle James, imprisoned Peter, and was later eaten by worms and died (Acts 12). Finally, his son Herod Agrippa II was the one before whom Paul appeared in Acts 25-26.

VIGNETTE 34
A SECOND CHANCE TO FOLLOW

Mark 10:17-22; Matthew 8:21; Luke 9:51-56; 14:25-33

Back in Capernaum, Jesus headed south along the Sea of Galilee down the Via Maris, arriving at one of the main docks that served the area. Several men stood awkwardly near the shore together, but their behavior indicated they were strangers to each other.

However, as Jesus greeted them, it was obvious each of them knew him. They returned his greeting respectfully, with a touch of wonder at seeing him.

One of the men, Mishael, took the lead. "Lord, it's good to see you alive and well, after what we heard from Jerusalem." He shifted his weight from foot to foot. "I must admit that I'm curious about why I was called to see you here today."

Hearing this, the other men perked up their ears. "What do you mean—called?" they asked.

Slightly abashed, Mishael responded, "Two nights ago, I had a dream in which an angel told me that I was to come to this place today, around three p.m. He said I would find something I'd been longing for."

The others considered his words. Then, the second man, Ananias, declared, "The same thing happened to me! A dream with an angel and the promise that if I came here, it would be beneficial for me."

The third, a Samaritan, spoke up, "I also saw an angel! But he told me that I'd have a chance to right a wrong I'd recently committed."

And the fourth, a tax collector friend of Matthew, added, "I, too, saw the angel. But he said what I learned today might cause me to change my job and my life."

Stunned by the similarity of their stories, the four men wondered how the angel's words would possibly come true.

Jesus watched their reactions, preparing to clarify the angel's message. After all, he had arranged for the angel to send them here today. As if by an unspoken signal, the four men turned with inquiring expressions to Jesus.

Jesus began, "Each of you had the opportunity to follow me in my ministry, learn from me, obey me, transform your lives. Yet each of you gave me different excuses why you couldn't.

"Mishael, you asked me what you needed to do to inherit eternal life. My Father revealed to me how you had lived, and I loved and respected you for it. Yet I said you lacked one thing; do you remember?"

Hanging his head, Mishael muttered, "I've not been able to forget it. You told me to sell everything I had, give it to the poor, and follow you. Everything else I do to obey the law now seems insignificant compared to the challenge you gave me. Yet, if I give away everything and follow you, what will I do? Who will I be? What I own has always been part of my identity. It's given me a position of importance in the town and allowed me to help many people."

Jesus nodded. "What you say is true, and your questions are important. I was thinking of you when I told the story about a man finding a pearl of great price. He sold everything to obtain the pearl.

What do you think the man did after that? He has a pearl, but nothing else!"

Mishael burst out, "Exactly! What would my wife and children say? Where would we live? What job would I have? I've felt paralyzed by the choice."

Jesus answered, "You're thinking more about what you would lose. Consider for a moment how the pearl could transform your life. What new opportunities would it give you? You're thinking more of yourself and your family. Consider more who my Father is, what he has planned for you, and how he might care for you."

Jesus saw the battle raging in Mishael's heart. He said gently, "My Father knows what needs you'll have. If you seek my Kingdom, he'll care for you in ways you can't imagine."

Jesus turned to Ananias. "You came to me one day, Ananias, and said you desired to follow me but needed to bury your father. That same day your friends also wanted to follow me, but one had just bought a field, another some oxen, another had just married."

Ananias was confused and somewhat defensive. "It was true! I did need to be with my family, and my friends had really done those things. Should we have ignored it all?"

"Those things *are* important," affirmed Jesus. "My Father was the one who gave you your families, jobs, possessions—and he wants you to be responsible with them.

"The key word holding you back is 'but.' It shows your mindset. Instead of looking for ways to obey and follow, you sought reasons to delay and refuse.

"When I said to people, 'If you do not hate your mother and father,' obviously, I didn't mean for them to despise and mistreat their families. Why would I want that, since they're blessings from my Father?

"Instead, I want them to seek first to follow and obey me, then adjust the rest of their lives to that most important commitment—not the other way around. Do you understand?"

Ananias studied the ground at his feet for a moment, then looked reluctantly at Jesus, nodding silently.

Jesus turned next to the Samaritan. Before Jesus said anything, the man spoke, "I understand now the meaning of the angel's words when he said I could right a wrong. At the time, I couldn't think of what it might be. Then, when I saw you, I remembered the day you and your disciples wanted to pass through our village, and we didn't let you."

Jesus grinned. "Some of my disciples were not too happy about it either. They thought for a moment they were Elijah." Turning serious, Jesus continued, "But of course, bringing fire was not what I wanted, so we went to the next village, which did receive us.

"Since then, Jehu, have you and your friends thought about why you were so reluctant to let us pass?"

Almost squirming, Jehu admitted, "I see now we were foolish, selfish, and short-sighted. Some of us resented how Jews had thrown us out when we tried to pass through villages in Galilee. We thought an eye for an eye was not only the proper response from the Law, but it also felt pretty satisfying!

"Some were afraid if we showed you hospitality, it would infuriate the Pharisees who opposed you. We already had enough trouble with them. Why would we seek more? And then, honestly, we thought perhaps we didn't deserve to have you come to our village."

His voice trailed off, and he was lost in thought for a moment. Jesus waited as the man pondered his words and was convicted by them.

Jehu turned back to Jesus, embarrassed yet relieved at finally unburdening his heart. "We were wrong. Hospitality and generosity mattered less to us than revenge and protecting ourselves." He met Jesus' eyes squarely. "Please forgive us, Lord. You'll be welcome the next time you come."

Jesus asserted, "I do forgive you. Thank you for your words. And whether I pass your way again, treat the next strangers who arrive at your village as if they were me. Will you do that?"

"I will!" affirmed Jehu.

Finally, Jesus addressed the fourth man. "Zedekiah! I met you first at Matthew's house, as one of his friends and colleagues. Then, I saw you listening many times in the crowd as I taught in Capernaum. Why do you think I wanted you to come today?"

Zedekiah replied, "Since the day you spoke about counting the cost of following you, I've struggled with what that could mean for me. I make a good living as a tax collector, although it doesn't win me many friends.

"Yet I can't escape the challenge—what would it mean for me to leave my job and follow you? Would the Romans be angry and punish me? Even if I weren't a collector anymore, would people ever accept or trust me? What other job could I find if they didn't? Or could I remain a tax collector and still love God and my neighbor?"

"I can tell you've thought about it," Jesus replied. "When someone considers going to war or building a tower, and the cost is too high, the answer is simply to not do those things.

"Yet when I tell you to count the cost of following me, I don't mean you shouldn't follow if the cost is high. Rather, I desire everyone to follow me. But they need to count carefully, as you have done.

"Following me will involve sacrifice, suffering, and uncertainty, but it also gives you access to blessings greater than you could ask or imagine. In me, you have a shepherd who will take care of you and relentlessly pursue you, even if you wander away or become lost. You have a Father who will forgive and love you even when you've disobeyed or been unwise.

"Yes, count the cost. But then come, follow me."

Jesus gathered the men close around him and sought out their eyes and hearts. "Let me ask you all now—were your reasons for not following me worth it?"

The men shook their heads.

"If you'd decided to follow me when you had the chance before, you would have already learned and benefited much."

They nodded, chastened.

"Yet my call is not given just once—it remains open to everyone, from now until the end of time.

"So, again, I invite you four to follow me, to commit fully to me. Choose the blessing, the pearl, the treasure, the opportunities. Not only that—go back to your homes and villages and invite everyone you know to do the same. In this way, you will be blessed, and others will also join the kingdom."

Reflect

1. When the man in Matthew 13 sold everything he had to buy the pearl, what did he do next? What did he tell his wife and family? Where did he sleep? Did he have to ask his friends for help? Was the pearl something he just hid away to have, or did it open other opportunities for him?
2. If Jesus told you that you lacked just one thing or had to give up just one thing in order to fully follow him, what would that thing be?

Learn

One of the top three study resources and best values I've found in all my years of ministry has been www.BiblePlaces.com, by Todd Bolen, which has more than 83,000 pictures from biblical lands, in jpeg or PowerPoint or Bible verse-by-verse format. They are from Israel,

After the Tomb

Jordan, Egypt, Lebanon, Iran, Iraq, Turkey, Greece, Italy, Europe, and many islands. these images include cities, mountains, rivers, objects, people, plants, animals, maps, and much more. They will bring color and life to your Bible study in unexpected, amazing ways. Even if you never went to any biblical land, this helps bring them to you.

Vignette 35
The Delivered Decapolis Demoniac

Mark 5:1-20; John 1:11; Matthew 15:29

Friday morning saw Jesus crossing the Sea of Galilee in the Spirit to the Decapolis, where the city of Hippos perched splendidly on a hill overlooking the Sea.

Soon, Jesus came to a small house where a man sat by the door, shaded from the morning sun. He was deep in animated conversation with several neighbors. Jesus stood watching for a moment, then the man became aware of the new visitor and turned to greet him.

Almost comically, an expression of sheer amazed joy came over his face, and he rushed to hug Jesus. He brought him to the circle of visitors and gave him his seat by the door as Jesus greeted the others present.

"This is the man who gave me back my life!" the man exclaimed to the group with pride and excitement. As Jesus listened, as a proud father might, Abishua continued his story to his friends about how Jesus had arrived one morning on the shore near the cemetery, confronted the demons Legion inside of him, and cast them out.

Though the story seemed almost too fantastic to believe, the evidence was literally standing in front of them. As Abishua finished his story, the guests asked him questions, then eventually stood, made their farewells, and walked away toward the center of the city.

Jesus laid a hand on the man's shoulder. "When a master returns from a journey, it's good for him to find his servant doing what his master gave him to do. It's obvious you took to heart the mission I gave you that day."

"Every moment of that morning is etched on my mind," Abishua answered. "After you delivered me from the demons, and people asked you to leave the country, I wanted so badly to go with you. Here, I thought I would be only the crazy man, the outcast, the dangerous one, the accursed.

"Yet you refused to let me go with you. I was surprised, disappointed, even a little hurt. You healed me, but didn't want me with you? Then you told me to return home and simply tell how much the Lord—you—had done for me."

Abishua reflected for a minute, while Jesus waited patiently. "I couldn't understand that day why the townspeople wanted you to leave, though I'm sure some of the owners of the pig herd were angry about losing their investment. But all you'd done was heal a man who no one had been able to help. I suppose they were scared by that since they didn't understand it.

"Though the town had cast me out, you accepted and freed me. Yet, they asked you to leave. It's ironic—the only ones cast out that day were the demons and you." Abishua shook his head.

Jesus inquired, "Tell me, what happened after you went home that day?"

Abishua paused for a moment, remembering the jumbled emotions he had felt—jubilation, gratitude, disappointment, trepidation. "When I got to this house, my wife and four-year-old son were waiting outside. They'd heard the story from friends of the pig herders but didn't know if it could be true.

"As I walked to the door, my wife was examining me from head to toe. I no longer had any wounds from the chains or rocks. I was calm, clothed, in my right mind—most of all, I felt at peace. She stepped forward hesitantly, looking deep into my eyes. She said later that my eyes convinced her that something had finally changed in me.

"She took a deep breath and put her hand on my cheek, her gaze still locked on me. Then she gently put her arms around me and her head on my chest and began to sob—but with tears of joy. And I was home." Abishua's voice broke as he recalled the tender emotions of that reunion.

"You gave me back my family! When my son saw that his mother wasn't scared, he came over and hugged our legs. I had regained everything that really mattered, and I was content."

Touched by the story, Jesus brushed a tear from his own eye, and said, "That's why I sent you back. Your story was to be for many people, but the first chapter was about you being made whole again in every way, starting with your wife and son. I'm so glad for you." Then Jesus asked him, "What happened in the town when you began to tell your story?"

Abishua laughed. "At first, it didn't go well at all. Though everyone had heard about me, most weren't convinced. I went into the center of town. People gave me a wide berth and hurried past, trying not to make eye contact. The mothers who had little children with them held their hands tightly as they passed or put the children on their side away from me.

"Finally, I heard a couple of young men on the corner making fun of 'the crazy man,' but what did I care about that? The man they were ridiculing didn't exist anymore. I walked toward them and asked them if they'd like to hear the crazy man's story. They shied away a little when I got close to them, but then one said, uncertainly, that he would.

"So, I told them! Like my guests just now, they found it hard to believe, but even harder to deny. As time went by, and I didn't scream or froth at the mouth or rip off my clothes," he grinned, "people began to look me in the eye, stop and talk, and listen to my story.

"After that first day, people lost most of their fear of me. One of the businessmen on the street invited me to his house the next night for dinner, and I told him my story. Soon, others did the same. I guess I was a novelty who intrigued them.

"The miracle of you casting out the demons got their attention. The next logical step for them was to wonder about what power enabled you to do that. And then they would ask me who you were.

"I told them I believed you were the Lord, that God was your Father, and he had sent you to help people like me. I told them you weren't like the other Jews who avoided Gentiles as if we were cursed. I believed you cared about us and wanted to help us.

"Many began to wonder, since you had healed me, if you could also heal them of the sicknesses they had. We had heard some stories from across the sea, but we didn't know if they were true. Even if they were true, would you do the same here?

Jesus praised him, "You've done well, Abishua! I'm proud of you. I know it was hard for you at first; but you've persevered and been so faithful. Because of you, many have come to faith. My Father has seen what you've done and will reward you for your courage and your testimony."

Abishua was moved by Jesus' words. "I was so glad when you came back later. I had told everyone I believed you would help them —*if* they didn't ask you to leave again!"

"True!" Jesus declared. "I'll never forget the day when at least four thousand came to see me outside this city. They were a testimony to your work."

"And you showed them your love and compassion, with healing and food," Abishua reminisced, "just as you had done for the Jews before."

Jesus nodded. "Abishua, in a few days I'll be going to Jerusalem, then back to my Father in heaven. I want you to continue telling your story here. Soon others will come from Jerusalem with news about a group of believers who are following me—they'll go first to the Jews, then to the Gentiles here. The Spirit of my Father will help direct them here. And you'll be my witness to them here and in all this region."

Abishua looked at Jesus soberly, trying to imagine what the future might hold. The past had already been completely unexpected and amazing. Then he knelt in front of Jesus and said humbly, "I am at your service. I owe you everything."

Jesus knelt beside him, put his hand on his shoulder, and prayed, "Father, thank you for Abishua and what you've done through him, starting that morning two years ago. Give him strength and wisdom. Open the hearts and minds of this city set on a hill so they will become your light in this land."

REFLECT

1. Jesus crossed the Sea of Galilee, calmed a storm, confronted the demons, and was eventually rejected and thrown out by the people of the town. Do you think he had planned to stay in the region longer, or that he knew what would happen, and went through all that to help just one person?
2. That day, he helped one man, but that one man eventually brought 4000 people or more to see Jesus. What one thing God is doing in your life that seems small now but could have unexpected, abundant results later on?

Learn

The region known as the Decapolis in the Bible had ten cities established by Alexander the Great, with Hellenistic values and patterns, that still remain in some form today as part of Jordan, Israel, and Syria. Their names then (and now) are: Canatha (Qanawat), Damascus, Dium (Capitolias), Gadara (Umm Qais), Gerasa (Jerash), Hippos, Pella, Philadelphia (Amman), Raphana (Abila), and Scythopolis (Beit She'an). Here is a good map to see them.

https://www.jw.org/en/library/books/Insight-on-the-Scriptures/Decapolis/

Vignette 36

The Circle Closes—Coming Near to God Again

Genesis 3:22-24; Exodus 33:7-11; 1 Kings 8:6-11; John 14:9; Hebrews 7:11-28

Jesus celebrated the third Sabbath after his resurrection by returning to the Capernaum synagogue. All those who had been present the week before had invited their friends from neighboring villages, so that the main hall of the synagogue was filled to the bursting point.

At Jairus' invitation, Jesus rose and requested three scrolls from the synagogue attendant. Jesus selected one and unrolled it to find the first passage.

"In the scroll of Genesis, we read the story of the first sin of Adam and Eve, and its consequences. The story ends: *'And the LORD God said, "The man has now become like one of us, knowing good and evil. He must not be allowed to reach out his hand and take also from the tree of life and eat, and live forever." So the LORD God banished him from the Garden of Eden to work the ground from which he had been taken. After he drove the man out, he placed on the east side of the Garden of Eden cherubim and a flaming sword flashing back and forth to guard the way to the tree of life.'"*

Jesus handed the scroll to the attendant and explained, "In the Garden, Adam and Eve enjoyed daily fellowship with my Father. In that perfect world, before the serpent came, they spoke face to face with my Father, clearly understanding his will and purposes. They had no concept of life outside that place or that relationship.

"But after their sin, human beings were suddenly distanced from God by their own disobedience and desires. The rest of the Tanakh describes how my Father has slowly closed the breach between humans and himself."

Taking the scroll of Exodus, Jesus read, *"Now Moses used to take a tent and pitch it outside the camp some distance away, calling it the "tent of meeting." Anyone inquiring of the* Lord *would go to the tent of meeting outside the camp. And whenever Moses went out to the tent, all the people rose and stood at the entrances to their tents, watching Moses until he entered the tent. As Moses went into the tent, the pillar of cloud would come down and stay at the entrance, while the* Lord *spoke with Moses. Whenever the people saw the pillar of cloud standing at the entrance to the tent, they all stood and worshiped, each at the entrance to his tent. The* Lord *would speak to Moses face to face, as a man speaks with his friend. Then Moses would return to the camp, but his young aide Joshua son of Nun did not leave the tent."*[1]

Jesus taught, "At first, my Father chose not to speak to everyone at once, but rather to one person, who would represent him to the rest. So, Moses received this privilege and responsibility. His experience restored part of what Adam and Eve enjoyed. Yet, it was incomplete—only part of the time in God's presence, and only one man talking with God."

Jesus found his next passage, *"Then the cloud covered the Tent of Meeting, and the glory of the* Lord *filled the tabernacle. Moses could not enter the Tent of Meeting because the cloud had settled upon it, and the*

---

1. Exodus 33:7-11 (NIV)

glory of the L*ord* *filled the tabernacle. In all the travels of the Israelites, whenever the cloud lifted from above the tabernacle, they would set out; but if the cloud did not lift, they did not set out—until the day it lifted. So the cloud of the* L*ord* *was over the tabernacle by day, and fire was in the cloud by night, in the sight of all the house of Israel during all their travels."*[2]

Jesus continued, "When the tabernacle was completed, the glory of God remained over the Most Holy Place, a visible reminder of the presence of God. Now instead of being outside the camp, God dwelt in the center of the camp, seen by all through the symbols of cloud and fire. Although God had moved closer, the people's experience of God was still incomplete, because only the high priest could enter the Most Holy Place, and that only once a year."

Jesus took the third scroll and read from Kings, *"The priests then brought the ark of the* L*ord's* *covenant to its place in the inner sanctuary of the Temple, the Most Holy Place, and put it beneath the wings of the cherubim ... When the priests withdrew from the Holy Place, the cloud filled the Temple of the* L*ord. And the priests could not perform their service because of the cloud, for the glory of the* L*ord filled his Temple."*[3]

Jesus gave the third scroll back to the attendant, then sat down in Moses' seat. "Now my Father chose a fixed location in a permanent building. People would always know they could seek his presence there. So, the Temple became the center of not only his presence but also the services, sacrifices, and feasts of the people. Yet still,l only one man could enter the presence of God, and only once a year.

"When the Temple was destroyed, and the people went into exile, they wondered if my Father had left them and whether the covenant was still in force. Though the prophets promised a return to the land, the presence of God once again seemed distant, or even absent.

"But then with the return of the exiles, the Temple was rebuilt,

---

2. Exodus 40:34-38 (NIV)
3. 1 Kings 8:6; 10-11 (NIV)

and all continued as before until about thirty years ago. At that time, my Father revealed the boldest, most unexpected part of his plan to come near his people. Not only would he send the promised Messiah, but also that Messiah would be God himself in the flesh, the Creator coming to the created.

"And so he sent me—the Word of God made flesh. During the last three years, while I've been teaching, healing, and working, you've seen the face of God himself among you. Day by day, without realizing it, you received the same privilege that Adam and Eve had in the Garden—to be in the very presence of God."

A buzz ran through the crowd as Jesus' words sank in. Jesus discerned their thoughts. God himself had returned to walk among them—and they had ignored him, argued with him, disobeyed him, and finally killed him. They were horrified and conscience-stricken. Would Jesus and his Father punish them, then leave them once and for all?

Jesus declared, "For all who receive me now and believe in me, my Father gives you the right to be children of God and live daily in his presence."

Relief swept the room as the potential punishment and abandonment disappeared. Then Jairus asked on behalf of the group, "But Lord, what will it mean for us to believe in you and follow you? What do you and your Father expect us to do?"

Jesus nodded. "I've already taught you some of what it means to be my followers and live in the Kingdom of heaven—how its citizens live, think, speak, and treat others.

"Now your understanding of the Law must change, and with it, some practices you've known your whole life. They have guided you to this point, and many of them served their purpose. For example, a high priest has always served as intercessor between God and his people. Now, my Father has made me High Priest forever. This change in the priesthood also means a change in parts of the law and covenant. I am the guarantee of the new covenant, the one who makes it possible through my identity and my actions.

After the Tomb

"My death in Jerusalem was a sacrifice for the sins of everyone who would believe in me and was a fulfillment of God's promise to Abraham to guarantee the covenant. Therefore, the sacrifices made to commemorate God's promises are no longer needed. The promises have been kept. All things in heaven and on earth have been purified by this perfect sacrifice. No more are required."

Jairus and the people were silent, trying to assimilate this difficult concept. Much of their religious life and the festivals had centered around bringing different offerings. Did that mean they didn't have to offer any sacrifices at all? Would other requirements replace the old ones?

"I know it's hard to understand," Jesus acknowledged. "But our people experienced something similar during the exile when they couldn't worship in the Temple or bring offerings to its altar. So, they offered their prayers, their study, and their deeds of compassion toward others, as the Law required. My Father accepted those things in place of the offerings commanded previously. Under this new covenant, it will be similar."

One of the synagogue elders asked, "We won't go to the Temple or offer sacrifices anymore?"

Jesus said, "My Father required those sacrifices for various purposes. For example, the animal sacrifices helped provide for the needs of the tribe of Levi and its priests. The sacrifices also taught the people about the gravity of sin, the importance of gratitude, and the discipline of giving generously. In these ways, they're part of the culture and spiritual education of the people, and so they could continue. But they're no longer related to salvation.

"In the same way, some of the laws regarding cleanliness or purity now gain a new focus. The core of purity for my Father has always been the heart—one's thoughts and desires, expressed in loving action. The laws regarding which foods are pure are no longer needed. All foods are clean. People can still observe these principles for their health, if they choose, but they are not required to be part of my Father's kingdom, nor will people be punished for what they eat."

Another man spoke up from the back. "How will we worship here in the synagogue or in the Temple? Will we lose our traditions or change how we worship?"

Jesus replied, "In the coming days, my Father will reveal more about how those who follow me will worship. Yet much of what you've known your whole lives will continue because many principles my Father gave in the Law remain the same.

"This is the core teaching: Worship the Lord your God with all your heart and soul. Praise him with a sincere heart, with joy and gladness, daily, in every way and place and manner available.

"You've expressed this in diverse ways through the centuries. At times, you used instruments like the harp or lyre, tambourine or trumpet, strings or flutes or cymbals. At times, you sang. Sometimes you danced. You worshiped alone, and you worshiped together. All of this will continue. Again, the most important part of worship is a heart willing to seek and praise my Father.

"During my time with you, you've been blessed to see how my Father has finished erasing the abyss between him and his people. God again lives among his people through me, and now also through you.

"Soon, my Father will reveal one more step of his plan to come near, fulfilling what Jeremiah promised regarding the new covenant. You will all receive permanently a blessing rarely given in the past. Be alert and ready for it! It will be 'Immanuel' for each one of you."

Reflect

1. What do you think the final step of God's coming closer is?
2. What is the most natural, authentic way you can worship or express your relationship to the Lord?

Learn

Consider some of the history and practices of Jewish worship in Psalms 66, 95, 96, 98, 100, 147-150; and the new covenant Jeremiah promised in Jeremiah 31:33-34.

Vignette 37

Lunch with the Rabbi of Nazareth

Luke 2:41-52, 4:14-30; 2 Corinthians 3:14-16

Early Sunday morning, Jesus moved in the Spirit to Nazareth to spend time with his family and townspeople he had known for decades. He joined those gathered for morning prayers in the Nazareth synagogue.

When the prayers were finished, people tarried to greet Jesus. Many seemed to study him covertly, yet searchingly, as if to convince themselves that this famous person was indeed the same Jesus who had grown up among them.

More than two hours later, everyone had left, and the local rabbi, Shemuel, invited Jesus to share the noonday meal with him. They walked down the street to the rabbi's small house.

Jesus gave thanks, "Blessed are you, King of the Universe, for planting this righteous man in this village and raising up a harvest of righteousness through him. I pray you bless and continue to use him to teach your Law, with ever-increasing understanding and wisdom."

Shemuel's eyes watered as he received this unexpected gift.

Jesus said, "I'm grateful for what you taught me as a boy in the synagogue. Your love for God and his Torah was evident to our group. You were a tree of life planted by streams of water for us."

Shemuel replied, "When your father and mother brought you to the synagogue school that first day, they entrusted you to me in the manner of one delivering a great treasure. I'll never forget your mother's eyes when she said, 'The Lord granted us the privilege of having this child in our family. He's taught us about the Lord. We trust that you'll also teach him about the Lord.'

"Of course, every child is precious in their own way, so I didn't think too much about it at the time. But when I began to teach you, it was as if your mind were already attuned to the Law, as if the Word were finding a home in you that somehow it was already familiar with—water running down channels already carved out …" His voice trailed off. "And I knew you were special.

"You were only five when you started classes, yet you seemed to glean meanings in some texts that the other children never considered. When we read and memorized the story of the Exodus of our people from Egypt, the other children talked about the meal. You asked about the blood of the lamb painted on the door. When the other children talked about the Angel of Death freeing the Hebrews, you asked how the Egyptian mothers felt about losing their firstborn children.

"Or when children talked about the Lord, they used the many names that described his character, actions, and identity—Shaddai, Rafael, Adonai, and more. You knew all those, of course, but often when you talked about the Lord, you simply said, 'My Abba.'"

Shemuel looked at Jesus. "Your mother was right! It was a rare privilege to sit with you at Adonai's feet."

"In some ways, I was just like the other children," responded Jesus. "I had to study hard to learn what you taught. And yet you're also right that I felt at home, as if the Word of God were my native language, or as if when I learned something new, it connected with something already present in my mind, an echo of words spoken before that was just now returning to be heard.

"As I grew, I recognized the voice in my head as the voice of my Father. From the time I went to Jerusalem at age twelve, my Father revealed more of his plan for me, teaching me about my true identity. He also showed me I must be completely obedient to his will, in spite of the suffering that would come."

There was a pause in the conversation, then Shemuel changed directions. "I'm glad to see that the service today ended differently than the one three years ago here!" His smile reflected genuine gladness, but also relief, mixed with a touch of embarrassed regret.

"That day, we didn't understand who you really were, nor what you were about to do. When you read from Isaiah and said that the scripture had been fulfilled, most of us thought you intended to teach and serve among the people, as many rabbis had. Who wouldn't be proud of such a fine young man?

"Of course, we all were certain that the Messiah, the *ntzer*, would one day come from our village. We had even named our town for that. But it had been hundreds of years since the village was given that name. In that time, many false Messiahs had come and gone.

"When you read that passage, we believed it referred to the Messiah, but it was hard for us to connect that with you. And when you criticized us for our lack of belief and praised Gentiles instead of Jews, we were angry."

Shemuel's thoughts went back to the crowd that day—quick-tempered, seething, ready to throw Jesus off the cliff outside town. "I'm ashamed to say I was also offended. As one who had taught you as a young boy, I felt it was disrespectful for you to speak of us in that way."

He sighed with regret. "I should've stopped the people, but I was still upset. However, God was watching over you and helped you walk away from us. Once you decided to leave, no one even tried to stop you. I never did quite understand how that happened—but I'm glad that it did!"

Jesus acknowledged, "When a prophecy is fulfilled, it's often difficult to recognize it at that exact moment. Despite all my parents and I had done to help the village while I grew up, there were always some who doubted. That was why I could never do many miracles here during my ministry. The community never fully recognized I am the Son of God and Messiah. Yet others, who did not have a veil over their eyes, recognized and affirmed my identity at once."

The rabbi nodded. "I understood more as I watched you these three last years. Someone would bring me a story about what you had taught, or someone you had healed, and then I would go home at night to pore over the scrolls of Isaiah, or the Psalms, or Zechariah. I slowly saw that what you did matched—and brought to life—what the prophets had said long ago. When you died, I grieved and wondered whether I had been mistaken—whether you were another well-meaning but misguided Messiah.

"But then came the news of your resurrection, and God again confirmed you as his Son and our Messiah. Even though many doubted before, now they believe."

Reflect

1. When do you think Jesus realized who he really was, and what his mission on earth would be?
2. Do you think Jesus could resist temptation, do miracles, and be perfect because he was divine or because he was a human who relied on God's help and power? If it was the latter, what does that mean for your ability to imitate Jesus in those ways?

Learn

At the time of Jesus, there were two basic kinds of rabbis—Torah teachers (teachers of the law) and rabbis with *semikhah* (*semicha*, authority)—each entitled to teach in their own ways and forms. See Ray Vander Laan's discussion of a rabbi and his disciples and how Jesus' education and ministry fit typical Jewish patterns.

https://www.thattheworldmayknow.com/rabbi-and-talmidim

Also see short videos about the Eastern mindset (class 12A), rabbis and *talmidim* (disciples, class 12B), and rabbinic teaching methods (class 12C) at

https://ibitibi.org/en/life-of-christ.

Vignette 38

Storytime Under the Olive Tree

Revelation 21:1-27; John 14:2-6

Late that afternoon, some of the villagers gathered near Nazareth's oldest olive tree. Some called it the namesake of the town, the reminder of the future.

The ancient tree had existed for hundreds of years. Its dogged endurance served as an apt testimony to God's eternal covenant with the nation of Israel. For generations, the town's rabbis and parents had brought the children here to teach them about Israel's history, and how God had brought them back to this place after the exile, his promises still in force.

On this pleasant evening, the Root of Jesse leaned against the trunk of the tree, the Promise now made flesh, complete. He watched with a smile on his face as the laughing children chased each other around the tree, climbing up and sitting in its branches, calling out to their parents.

Eventually, they grew tired, and like moths drawn to a flame, they gathered around Jesus, one claiming a spot on his lap, the others crowding as close as they could. One of the children said, "Tell us a story!"

Jesus smiled at the circle of bright faces and said, "In just a few days, I'll be leaving Galilee and going home."

One child said, "What home? I thought you grew up here."

Jesus replied, "I did live here for a while. But before that, I lived far away. In fact, it's so far away that you can't get there in a thousand days, even if you rode the fastest horse!"

The children goggled at him, eyes wide. "Then how can we get there?"

"Well," he replied. "I guess you could say that I'm the way to get there—you have to walk with me. In fact, my Father wants all of you and your families to come. He's getting everything ready for you to come, if you want to."

"But is it a fun place? What can we do there?" inquired one young boy.

Jesus looked at the children. "What do you like to do?" he asked. The answers poured out enthusiastically.

"I like to climb trees!"

"I like to swim in the ocean!"

"I want to play games with friends!"

"I like to *eat*!"

Jesus laughed and promised them, "Where I live, you can do all that!" He raised his eyes and asked the parents gathered around, "And if you could go there, what would you want to do?"

Some of them looked a little embarrassed, as if too old to take part in a children's fantasy game. Others grew thoughtful as they pondered.

Finally, a young mother said, "I'd like to be sure my children would have a safe place to grow up and never be hurt."

A father added, "I'd like to know I could provide enough for my family, and even extra."

An older woman said, "I'd like to be able to do what I did when I was younger—and never get old again!"

After the Tomb

A young man said, "I would want to create something new and amazing that would be beautiful and useful to people."

Jesus listened to their words and hearts—the worry, the longing, the despair, the eagerness, the passion—then said quietly, "Where I'm going, you can have all those things."

Now even the adults were wide-eyed, though some looked doubtful or uncertain.

Jesus continued, "Let me tell you a little about my true home. In one place," he said, looking at the boy who wanted to climb trees, "there's a tall mountain covered with trees and a stream rushing down the mountainside into a beautiful lake below. Around the lake is a wonderful valley, with fields and meadows and a forest of trees on which grow all kinds of fruits and nuts. Every kind of bird and animal live in the fields and forest, and the lake has every sort of fish you can imagine—and even some you can't!

"My Father lives in a splendid, enormous palace, in the middle of a fabulous city built on a mountain at the other end of the valley. The walls of the city are of white marble, and the streets of the city are like pure gold. The gate of the city is of the finest cedar wood, decorated with the most precious and colorful gems set in silver and mounted on it.

"Those who live in my Father's country are always happy and secure." Jesus glanced over at the young mother. "They love my Father and each other. They take care of each other and share everything they have.

"In my Father's country, people are never bored. There are always interesting things to do. Every day they invent ways to make the city more interesting or beautiful—build new houses or buildings, write stories or songs, create fun games, paint pictures, or make sculptures.

"Every night people go to the palace for a great banquet with all the best foods and dishes. Then they take turns showing each other what they've done that day and let people try their new inventions.

"They tell stories about what they did that day, or about their time on earth. Or my Father tells them stories they've never heard about people from places they've never been.

"Occasionally, my Father invites some of the citizens to do something entirely new." Jesus smiled at a young boy next to him. "How would you like to help my Father invent a new animal that no one has ever seen?"

The boy's eyes sparkled. "Could I really? Yes!"

Jesus asked the girl on his lap. "And you—how would you like to fly through the air like the birds, wherever you wanted?" The girl looked up and nodded shyly as Jesus smiled at her.

The adults chuckled indulgently as they watched their children. Jesus repeated, "Where I'm going, you can have and do all these things." The children gazed at him in wonder-full belief. The adults hesitated. They wanted it all to be true, but it seemed too distant, too unlike their present reality. Skepticism and hope competed in their eyes.

Jesus said gently to them, "If this were not so, I would have told you. I'm going there to prepare a place for you. If you believe in me, I'll come back and take you all to be with me there. Remember, I am the way to my Father's country. I want every one of you to be there.

"I know it seems as if that place is far away, in space and in time. Yet if you're part of the kingdom which I've told you about for three years, then you're already citizens of my Father's country. You've started to live in his kingdom, though it may not really seem like it yet.

"Whenever you love me or my Father, you prove you're part of our kingdom. When you share with each other, take care of each other, teach each other, have fun together, have a good meal—you're getting a taste of what living in my Father's country will always be like. So, live in this way, until I come back to take you there."

Reflect

1. How do you understand the passages about heaven in Revelation, such as chapters 21-22? What can or should be taken literally, or what should be taken symbolically?
2. Of the things mentioned in this reflection, what would you most look forward to in heaven?

Learn

I highly recommend Randy Alcorn's book, *Heaven,* for its teaching about what heaven may be like, including what our bodies will be like, what we may do, what our relationships may be like, and much more. A key concept is that of redemptive continuity—the idea that God will redeem his creation, so that everything good he created for earth will continue in some way in heaven.

Vignette 39

Would You Like to Write a Gospel?

John 14:26, 15:26, 16:13-15; Mark 12:41-44; 1 Kings 17

By mid-morning on Monday, Jesus was back in Capernaum. He went first to Peter's house and greeted his family, as well as John, who had spent the night there.

Jesus said to John, "Come with me. I want to discuss something with you."

John eagerly followed him out of the house and down the street to Matthew's house in the northern part of the village. Jesus repeated his invitation to Matthew, then led them to the synagogue.

The village rabbi and Jairus were in the main hall of the synagogue, talking together. After greeting them, Jesus asked, "May my friends and I talk together in the synagogue school? We'll be gone by the time the students arrive this afternoon." The rabbi gladly assented.

The three gathered around a table, remembering when they had spent hundreds of hours studying the Torah in places like this—John in Bethsaida, Matthew in Capernaum, Jesus in Nazareth.

Jesus asked them, "When you studied the Torah and the

Prophets, did you ever think about the men who wrote those books, or how they wrote them?"

John replied, "I used to wonder how God chose them. Were they the best students or writers? Or were they more righteous? Or maybe they were eyewitnesses?"

Matthew added, "I supposed God just chose whoever he thought was best for each book. But I wondered how they decided what to write. Did God dictate to them, like the rabbis did with us sometimes? Did they just write what they saw, or their favorite stories or ideas? Did they talk to other people to learn from them, or did they write it by themselves?"

"Good questions!" Jesus commented. "My Father did choose people who loved him and cared about sharing his stories with other people. No writer was perfect. No one knew every detail about everything, and no one wrote with exactly the same style.

"These men of faith prayed to my Father as they were writing, and he helped them remember things they had seen or studied. When an author was not an eyewitness to an event—like the creation or the flood—then my Father led him to sources that had preserved those stories. Yet, my Father allowed each author to maintain their own perspective. That's why some of the Writings like the Books of Kings, Chronicles, or Samuel are different in some details.

"When people experience the Word of God, it's living and active. That means that each person might understand or apply the Word a little differently. And since people's life situations and perspectives have changed throughout history, the constant challenge is to apply the Word of God in the most relevant way possible.

"My Father reveals himself and truth in every part of the scriptures. Since my Father is unlimited in time or space or knowledge, he'll always reveal something new in his Word to those who seek him.

"That's partly what David meant when he said, 'Show me your ways, O Lord; teach me your paths; guide me in your truth ... the Lord confides in those who fear him; he makes his covenant known to them.'

"So, my Father helps the different authors teach something new to those who seek him. Taken together, they paint a multi-faceted picture of Him. This is why those who believe in my Father and follow him can't do so on their own. No one can understand all the Word of God by themselves. They need a community, because each person contributes something new and useful, and together the community continually grows in their understanding of the Word and my Father."

There was a lull as Matthew and John considered Jesus' words. From next door, they heard the quiet voices of the rabbi and Jairus, and from outside, the sounds of a bustling morning in the village.

Jesus resumed, "Much of this you've already considered. But I mention it again to ask you both, would you like to join them?"

Caught off guard, the two men looked at each other in confusion, then back at Jesus. Matthew asked, "Join who? In what?"

Jesus smiled. "Join the authors who wrote the Word you've studied your whole life."

Their faces were still blank. They weren't tracking at all. John ventured, "I don't understand. How would we join them?" He looked around the room. "Are they ... here somewhere?"

Jesus chuckled. "No; but in a few days, those who believe in me will enter a new era in their lives. At Mount Sinai, the Israelites began to live under a different covenant than the one God made with Abraham. In the same way, my followers will share in a new covenant based on my life, death, resurrection, promises, and power.

"Just as my Father provided the Law in written form, my followers will eventually need a record of what I've done." He searched their eyes in turn. "I want you to write about my story—my good news."

Matthew and John were stunned. All their lives they had revered the Word of God, studied it, memorized it, meditated on it, wondered about the men who had written it. Now Jesus was asking them to join Isaiah, David, Jeremiah, and so many others in sharing the story of salvation—a story that now culminated in the Son of God coming to live with humans. Not only had they lived part of the story—now they would also write it!

Gradually recovering from the shock, Matthew and John considered how they would achieve this. John queried, "Do you mean that you want us to write the story together?"

"No," replied Jesus. "Each of you is different. Matthew, your job has taught you to be organized and methodical, to be able to present a clear report of what you do. You're used to reconciling different accounts from businesses with your own work. These traits will serve you well as you set out to give an account of what you've lived with me.

"As a faithful Jew, you know what your brothers and sisters expect from the prophecies about the Messiah. You'll be reconciling their expectations with the reality of my ministry among them. You'll help them understand how my Father has kept the promises made throughout the scriptures."

Jesus turned to John. "John, one of your gifts is your passion, even though sometimes it's misdirected into anger or pride. You've begun to learn how to love the way I taught all of you. You're perceptive and open to the Spirit, willing to believe and to act. You have a gift for making loyal friends. So, what you write will be different from Matthew's writing and will be helpful to a different audience. People far from here—both in distance and in beliefs—will come to faith in me because of what you write.

"I'm not choosing you because you have perfect faith or actions or character—though you have some of all three. Rather, I choose you because I believe in you. And remember, I've promised to send the Spirit to teach and remind you in this new responsibility as well—just as my Father aided the writers of the Tanakh. You've been eyewitnesses to much of my ministry, but my Father will also reveal to you details that you could not have known about some of those stories.

"Others will pass down many stories, perhaps even private events of my ministry for which you were not present. In the next several years, you'll have time to choose what stories you'll include, reflect on what you believe my Father wants you to say, and select the main audience with whom you want to share your stories.

"The truth is," Jesus finished, grinning at John, "if you tried to write down all the stories of the people I have been with, there might not be enough room in the world for all of them!

Reflect

1. What is the balance between God inspiring biblical authors with his truth, and him allowing them to write from their own perspectives and background? Some would say God permits apparent contradictions or errors in some of the historical writings like Kings, Chronicles, and the Gospels. How would you respond?
2. How might such questions impact your faith in or understanding of the Bible?

Learn

The three major divisions of the Jewish Old Testament were the Torah (Law), the Navim (Prophets), and the Ketuvim (Writings). The Jews combined the first letter of each of these sections and formed the word Tanakh, which is their word for the Old Testament. In fact, for many Jews who do not believe in Jesus as the Messiah, they do not accept the New Testament as their Bible. They don't have the Old and New Testaments, but rather just the Tanakh. Also, some of the books in the Hebrew Tanakh are combined differently than our Old Testament. For example, 1-2 Samuel are one book, as are 1-2 Kings and 1-2 Chronicles. What we call the 12 Minor Prophets are one book in the Tanakh. This type of change results in a total of 24 books in the Hebrew Tanakh, not 39 books as many accept it.

For more information about the Hebrew Bible, see https://en.wikipedia.org/wiki/Hebrew_Bible#:~:text=In%20Tiberian%20Masoretic%20codices%2C%20including,%2C%20Esther%2C%20Daniel%2C%20Ezra

Vignette 40

Get out of the Boat!

Psalm 89:9, 107:29-30; Job 9:8; Hebrews 12:2; John 14:12

Tuesday morning dawned bright and sunny, the air fresh and filled with the aroma of new flowers, spring fully arrived. Jesus met the disciples outside the synagogue after the morning prayers.

"Let's go to the boat. I have something special to do with you all today." They walked together down to the main dock of Capernaum, where a boat was ready to put out to sea.

Since the morning was still, they rowed out to the middle of the lake, heading toward Bethsaida on the northern shore. When still some distance away, Jesus told them to stop rowing. The boat coasted through the water, then rocked gently as it slowed to a stop.

It was a perfect day. Tiny waves slapped against the bow of the boat, birds darted and turned overhead, the fishing villages drowsed peacefully on the shores of the lake, sparkling in the morning sun.

"Peace, be still," murmured John. "And it is ..."

"You know many people believe this sea is a place where pagan gods or demons have power to stir up storms or sink boats," Jesus declared to them. "Some even call it 'the abyss,' believing that beneath this sea is an opening to Hades. But in our time together, you've seen that God ultimately controls all of it. After I stilled the storm, you asked each other, 'Who is this that commands even the winds and the waves?'

"Remember the psalms: *'You rule over the surging sea; when its waves mount up, you still them,'* and *'He stilled the storms to a whisper; the waves and the sea were hushed. They were glad when it grew calm ...'*[1] Jesus smiled at them. "And you were glad!

"Then the night when I came to you walking on the water, you thought I was a ghost. But remember Job's words, *'God alone stretches out the heavens, and treads on the waves of the sea.'*"[2]

He paused to scan their thoughtful faces. "That first night after the storm, you began to catch a small glimpse of who I was. You've witnessed me do things which before only my Father could do. So, you're experiencing one of my names—Immanuel. God with you, right now, in this boat. When God is with you, all things are possible."

The silence that ensued seemed like a dream from which they would awake—yet it was no dream. Silently they replayed the events of those two occasions—fear being replaced by awe, imminent disaster converted to impossible miracles. And the most improbable miracle of all sat smiling at them from the front of the boat—God made flesh.

Seeming to switch topics, Jesus remarked, "Sometimes, while we were walking on the road, I heard you talking among yourselves about who was the greatest." They looked at each other a little shamefacedly. "At least once," Jesus continued, "I heard Peter asking whether any of you had ever walked on water, like he had. Even though you didn't like it, that ended the conversation."

Peter gave a small chuckle.

---

1. Psalm 89:9 (NIV)
2. Job 9:8 (NIV)

"So," said Jesus briskly, "would you like to try?" He looked at them expectantly. They gazed back, puzzled. Then suddenly, they understood, and he saw eagerness spark in some of their eyes.

Peter cleared his throat. "If anyone needs me to show you how to do it again," he ribbed them gently, "I'd be glad to go first!"

Jesus extended his hand with a flourish over the side of the boat toward the water. "By all means, Peter. But let me be ready, just in case." Calmly, Jesus stepped out of the boat, strolling casually several paces away. Then, he turned back to them. The other disciples gasped. Even though they had seen this before, somehow, it seemed even more unreal in the morning sun.

Standing up, Peter stretched. "A calm morning instead of a stormy night. This should be pretty easy." With one final smirk back toward the other men, Peter took a large step over the edge—and plummeted straight under the water with a great splash. Seconds later, he surfaced, thrashing around, spluttering, reaching for the boat blindly. Showing mercy, John and James grabbed his hands and hauled him back into the boat amid shouts of laughter and joking.

"Peter the Rock sinks straight to the bottom!"

"You don't have to dive for the fish. We have nets for that!"

"Thanks for showing us, Peter, but we already know how to drown!"

Jesus laughed as he watched his friends. Who would have thought three years ago this group would ever be as close as they had become?

Jesus grinned mischievously at Peter and called out. "That won't be hard to beat! Who's next?"

Suddenly as still as the waters, the men looked around, each wanting the others to step up. Then, surprisingly, Thomas stood up. "I'll try! But how do I do it?" he asked Jesus.

"Just take the first step and trust me. Look at me—not at them, not at the water, not thinking you can't do this." He lowered his voice as if only for Thomas. "Stop doubting and believe!"

Thomas hesitated a moment, one foot in the bottom of the boat, one on the edge. At last, fixing his eyes resolutely on Jesus, he pushed off and stepped out and down, and his foot landed surely and solidly on the water. It was as if he were walking on dry land. Never once taking his eyes off Jesus, he covered the distance confidently, walking into Jesus' open arms. The men in the boat erupted in cheers, impressed, yet finding it hard to believe that Thomas, of all people, had done it.

Stepping back from the hug, Jesus took him by both shoulders and reminded him gently, "See what happens when you believe? The next time the father of lies tells you something is impossible, remember this moment. Nothing my Father wants you to do will be impossible for you."

Then both turned toward the boat. "Who's next?" they shouted together.

One by one, now jostling to respond, the men stepped out of the boat. Some went completely under, like Peter, and were helped back into the boat to try again. Others started well but gradually sank deeper and deeper until being rescued by Thomas and Jesus. Eventually, each of them found their "sea legs" and made their way to Jesus.

When the last one arrived, the group stood there, incredulous. How could this be possible? They shook their heads and laughed together out of pure joy, pounding each other on the shoulders, hugging each other and Jesus exuberantly.

Gradually, they calmed down. The empty boat sat rocking placidly on the water while they stared at it. Jesus said, "I told you that you'd do the works I've done. This is only a small example. Remember that you've already done other works like mine—preaching, healing, cleansing the lepers, and casting out demons.

"These are the things that God my Father has done. I am the Son of God and have done what my Father does. While you are *not* God, you're made in the image of God. Because you believe in me, God is pleased to call you his children. Because the Spirit lives in you, you'll be able to do anything my Father wants you to do.

"Remember that most things my Father calls you to do will require that same first step of faith—in the face of doubt, experience, ridicule by others, outright unbelief, or rejection of God.

"Yet, when you take the first step, look what can happen!" Jesus pointed at the boat. "You're standing the middle of a lake looking at a boat!"

They burst out laughing, full of amazement.

"Remember also that the safest place to be in a storm is near my Father and me. No boat, no building, no city, no place, no object in itself provides safety." He paused, looking at each one to emphasize his message. "And even if you're with me, you'll still suffer hardships at times. Yet if you remain with me, in the end, you'll be safe—and saved."

They nodded as his words penetrated deeply, carving out a place to remain in their hearts for the rest of their lives. They would never forget this moment, and they would often tell the story.

Then they glanced around at each other again and down at the water beneath their feet, seeing the fish swimming back and forth under them. Laughter rang out again as they walked—*walked!*—back toward the boat to finish their trip.

Reflect

1. Jesus promised that anyone who has faith in him will do the things he had done, and even greater things (John 14:12). What does that include? Is anything excluded?
2. What personal motivations would you have for getting out of the boat or staying in it?

Learn

Doug Ponder has an insightful article connecting the events of John 6 (feeding of the 5000 and walking on the water) with the events of the Exodus (Passover, manna in the desert, and crossing the Red Sea). He also discusses the symbolism of the sea in the Bible.

https://tabletalkmagazine.com/posts/why-did-jesus-walk-on-water-2020-03/

Vignette 41

A Special Wedding in Caesarea Philippi

Mark 9:14-27; Matthew 15:21-28

On Thursday morning, Peter, James, and John followed closely behind Jesus as they walked through Caesarea Philippi, intrigued by the mysterious appointment awaiting them. He turned and approached a house on the corner. The front door stood open, and sounds of laughter and happy conversation drifted out into the street. Jesus strode confidently up to the door, gave a brisk knock, and called out, "We're here! Is lunch ready?"

The four people sitting at the table jumped to their feet and came quickly to greet them in a blur of happy hugs and introductions.

"I brought my friends to meet you today," said Jesus, nodding at each of his disciples in turn. "Peter, James, and John—meet my friends, Paulus and his son Lucas, and also my friends Alara and her daughter Daphne." Jesus could sense the question in his disciples' minds as to who these four were and why they had come to meet them.

Recognition and comprehension dawned on John's face as he

finally placed them, out of the thousands of faces of Jesus' ministry. "We saw you here before on the mountain when ..." he glanced at Jesus, "you came to ask Jesus to heal your son!"

Peter and James were amazed at the change in the boy. That day on the mountain, the demons had tormented Lucas and thrown him to the ground in a convulsion, mouth foaming. Now, he was calm, reserved, clean and well-dressed, with a pleasant demeanor and a confident spirit.

Then James, spurred by the memory of that encounter, realized who the mother and daughter must be. With a mixture of wonder and excitement, he asserted, "And you're the woman who came to see Jesus near Tyre!"

Alara nodded, with a slightly ironic smile. "I am, though at that time, you weren't so willing to receive us." Chastened, the three disciples remembered they had urged Jesus to send the woman away.

"You're right," John said frankly. "I'm embarrassed to remember our rudeness. Please forgive us. We often said things we shouldn't have."

Alara responded graciously, "Jesus has blessed each of us in ways we don't deserve. Now is not the time for guilt but rather for gratitude. Please, all of you, come. Let's share our stories over a meal."

They gave thanks for the food and ate as Paulus shared his story with them. "Here in Caesarea Philippi, we had heard about a man who was healing and teaching in Galilee. Yet such stories were common. Often, they were just lies or wishful thinking. Even if the stories were true, who would receive us in Capernaum or Bethsaida? We knew the Jews there considered all of us from this mountain as unclean pagans.

"But then word came that you had gone to Tyre and Sidon and had healed a young girl who was demon-possessed. Was it possible you might heal Lucas too? I was at my wit's end. Desperate, I took him to see if I could find Alara, and she shared her story with me."

Alara picked up the narrative, "When I begged you to heal Daphne, I knew you had no obligation to help us, but I had heard you were a man of compassion who showed great love for children."

"You showed great faith!" Jesus affirmed her. "Even though you're not a Jew, you sensed the truth about my Father's generosity. It's not measured in leftover crumbs, nor does he consider Gentiles dogs, as you might have thought. Rather, he is a God of such abundance that he has more than enough blessings to share with all."

Jesus turned to her young daughter and gently touched her cheek. "And I was happy to help you, Daphne." She ducked her head shyly but peeked up at Jesus in trusting wonder.

Paulus resumed, "When I heard their story, I hoped it might be possible for you to free Lucas also. We traveled here as quickly as possible. People said you'd been in town but had left several days before to go to the mountain with your disciples, so I set out to find you.

"We found your disciples, yet they couldn't help us—then you arrived! By then, I was almost panicking, thinking that my last chance of helping my son was about to disappear." His voice caught, still vividly remembering the desperation choking him during those moments, fueled by the powerful demons who maliciously tortured his son.

"I know my faith was small. I did believe in you, because of Alara and Daphne! But Lucas' suffering had lasted for years. It seemed too much to hope that he would be freed, and we could return to a normal life."

Jesus replied, "I knew you were struggling, yet you did exactly what I wish every tormented person would do—you asked me to help you in your weakness. A humble heart that longs for God's help will always receive his grace.

"I was grieved by the attacks Lucas had suffered for so long. Living near a stronghold of the devil had exposed him to danger. Some people who are old enough to choose their own path invite the devil to exercise his power on them, though they rarely realize clearly what they have done. But with Lucas, I knew he was still too young to make such a decision, and I wanted to protect him. So, I told the demons to go away and never enter him again."

Paulus resumed, "When I came back to town, everyone celebrated with Lucas and me. I sent word to Alara and Daphne and thanked them for helping me. It's only been a few months since Daphne and Lucas were healed. Since then, Alara and I have spent time together and realized how much we have in common."

Alara smiled shyly at Jesus. "We've decided to get married! When we heard you had been raised from the tomb, we hoped we would see you again."

Peter, James, and John were caught off guard by the announcement, then smiles broke out on their faces. "That's wonderful!" they exclaimed.

"I told my disciples that my Father had arranged this meeting," grinned Jesus. "I meant not only today, but also your two families coming to know and love each other. I'm happy for you! Congratulations!"

Paulus took a deep breath. "Since you were the one who brought us together, and healed our children, would you also perform our marriage ceremony while you're here? We don't want anything large or fancy. We don't have many people to invite. We just want you to bless our marriage."

"I'd be honored to," beamed Jesus. The afternoon passed quickly as the group prepared for a simple wedding, inviting neighbors and asking several women from the neighborhood to cook a simple meal.

About sunset, everyone gathered around a small wedding tent. The couple stood in front of Rabbi Jesus, with Daphne and Lucas by their parents. The disciples took up their places near Paulus, while several of Alara's friends stood near her.

A hush fell on the group. Jesus closed his eyes in silent meditation, as did the couple. The silence deepened till it seemed even the birds had gone silent, and the usual evening sounds had disappeared. Only a small breeze rustled through the nearby trees.

Jesus took a deep breath and said, "Father, in the beginning you made Adam and Eve in your image. You knitted them together to help each other and to work in the garden. We now ask you to do the same for Paulus and Alara. You've rescued them and their children from the damage done by the Deceiver. Now join them as husband and wife and bring your complete *shalom* on them and the home they begin today. Amen."

They all opened their eyes. Jesus paused a moment and smiled down at Daphne and Lucas. Eyes wide and sober, they looked at him, then at their parents. Jesus stretched out a hand to each of them. They took his hands and he prayed again, "And Father, bless Daphne and Lucas in a special way too. Protect them from the Deceiver. Place your Spirit in them, so they always know how much you love them and how important they are."

Jesus turned his gaze on the couple. "Today you start a new chapter as a family, with all the changes that will bring. I proclaim my blessing on you both as you learn to live together, as the Lord wants you to do.

"I also challenge you and all those who've believed in me because of your witness to them. You've lived for years in the shadow of the temples and altars above this town. You've seen the sacrifices and the pagan practices, and some of you took part in them. The name of that cave, the 'Gates of Hades,' is well-deserved. The Deceiver has had far too much influence, far too many victories here.

"My Father and I defeated Satan and cast his demons out of Daphne and Lucas. He no longer has any power over them. My Father and I have counterattacked against Satan in this very place, at the gates of hell. I've begun to build my church here—and the gates of hell will not overcome it!"

The people murmured to each other. They had not understood the spiritual battle being waged, nor who the participants were, nor how the two healings were related to the pagan complex at the edge of town.

"Now, I call upon all of you to be witnesses in this town. Accept each other, help each another, take care of each another, learn from one another, protect and serve one another. Then go out and tell the rest of the town what my Father and I have done. Don't be afraid to go even to the temples, the altars, the cave, and share the story with them as well. Many there are confused, but they'll listen and follow me. Yet others will not. They'll be angry and lash out at you.

"When that happens, remember that my Father and I will be with you, guide you, and strengthen you. If you remain faithful to us and help one another, then the gates of hell will not overcome you."

Reflect

1. What do you believe about the power of Satan to influence, tempt, control, or possess people today? In what specific ways might he gain such access or control?
2. Assuming that this is possible for him, how can you be protected from being hurt by him, or help protect the people you love?

Learn

The confession of Peter about Jesus at Caesarea Philippi, in Matthew 16:13-28, is a famous story from the gospels. I recommend Ray Vander Laan's excellent DVD series of Faith Lessons (16 volumes). Of these, volume 4, video lesson 3 tells this story relevant to its cultural and geographical context, with great effect and impact.

Vignette 42

More than Five Hundred—the Galilean Believers

Luke 1:76-79; John 15:1-25; Matthew 24:31;
1 Corinthians 15:51-52; Philippians 1:6

Early Friday morning, Jesus gathered his apostles and the women of his traveling group around him. "This afternoon will be a special time—one you'll remember the rest of your lives," he began. The disciples listened, intrigued. But then, much of what had happened in the last three years fell in that category. "I want you to go throughout Capernaum and the villages nearby. Tell the people that at midafternoon, I'll meet you all on Mount Eremos, the place where I've taught them, fed them, and healed many."

Mystified, yet excited, the group scattered in pairs, some heading north and others south on the Via Maris. By late morning, the message had been delivered, and the disciples set out for the mount overlooking the Sea. About midafternoon, they came up the hill, gratefully stretching out on the soft green grass.

A steady stream of people arrived. From the north, people from Capernaum and Bethsaida left the road and climbed up to them. Others came over the crest of the mount from the direction of

Chorazin, and yet others straggled in from villages on the lake to the south, from Magdala, Gennesaret, and Tiberias.

Jesus watched as they joined the group of disciples. Though tired from their unanticipated journeys, they were smiling and hugging one another as long-lost friends or relatives at an unexpected reunion. Jesus walked among the crowd, greeting most of them, and they received him with the affection, reverence, and respect reserved for a king.

There were Jairus and Fulvia with their daughter, Rebecca; Daniel, the boy who shared the loaves and fishes, his mother, and his siblings; Marcus the centurion and his servant, Theo; Peter's mother-in-law, Hannah; Zebedee's clan; and Eliab, the official from Capernaum and his son, Abishai. Also present were a host of those whom Jesus had healed, such as the paralytic and his family from Capernaum, and Seth, the former blind man from Bethsaida. These and many more had followed Jesus all around Galilee as he taught in their synagogues and villages, stayed in their homes, ate at their tables, and healed their sick.

What Zechariah, the father of John the Baptist, had prophesied about Jesus and John, as well as Malachi, had been fulfilled with these people. They had been living in darkness, and the shadow of death, yet the rising sun had shone on them, infused them with hope, and guided them into the path of peace. They had come today, more than five hundred of them, to listen once again to this rabbi. He had demonstrated the mercy, forgiveness, salvation, and love of the Father in tangible ways they had never experienced before.

Gradually the crowd settled down, conversations trailing off as they saw Jesus stand before them. Soon it was so still, the only sound was the soft breeze moving through the grass and the distant lapping of the waves on the shore.

"Many of you were here three years ago when I began to teach you about my Father's Kingdom," said Jesus. "Do you remember the story I told you at the end of my message that day?" He paused and

After the Tomb

let his gaze wander around the group. Several nodded, murmuring words indistinctly.

One young woman spoke up. "You said if we listen to your words and put them into practice, we would be like a wise man who builds his house on the rock. But those who don't practice them are foolish, like one who builds on the sand where their house can be swept away."

"Exactly!" approved Jesus. "Those of you here today have shown yourselves to be wise. You've chosen to follow me and learn from me, then to live what I taught. You're among the first citizens of the Kingdom.

"Soon, my Father will send the Spirit to organize and launch a new group of believers in Jerusalem, and my apostles will lead it. It will spread quickly throughout the country. You will be the pioneers of that new movement here in Galilee, witnesses who imitate what I did during my ministry.

"Today, I want to tell you some of what I shared with my disciples four weeks ago. I am the vine, and you are the branches. If you remain in me, and I in you, you'll bear much fruit. Apart from me, you can do nothing. If you keep my commands, you'll remain in my love. Love each other as I have loved you.

"If you do the same things I have done—teach, love, serve—you're truly my disciples. Some people will believe you, just as they believed me. If they obeyed my teaching, they'll obey yours also. But others will reject and persecute you just as they rejected and persecuted me.

"So don't be discouraged. Rather, persevere even in suffering. Remember what I told you earlier on this mountain—if you're persecuted because of righteousness, you're blessed. Rejoice and be glad, for great is your reward in heaven.

"Don't be confused by false leaders who will arise to distract you from the real kingdom, but rather hold fast to my teaching. Your battle is not against the Romans or the Zealots, the Pharisees or Sadducees, but against the Accuser who lies, steals, destroys, and kills. Against him, your most effective weapons will be truth, kindness, light, and faithfulness. You've seen those qualities. Therefore, imitate me, and the Accuser will be defeated.

"Be alert and prepared not only for the end of Jerusalem but also the end of the world when all my Father's enemies will be destroyed. Just as on Rosh Hashanah the trumpet announces the new year, a trumpet will also sound at the end of the world, and the Son of Man will send his angels to gather his elect from the four winds. The dead will be raised, and the judgment will take place. Those who have been faithful to me will enter into the joy of my Father's eternal kingdom—the inheritance prepared for them since the creation of the world.

"See, I've told you ahead of time. Don't be alarmed or surprised. Instead, be watchful and prepared."

Jesus' disciples and the five hundred listened breathlessly, unwilling to take their eyes off Jesus even for a moment. Hearts deeply pierced, they were intensely aware of every sound, word, color, and movement. The recent events in Jerusalem, which had seemed like the end of Jesus' ministry, now were clearly the prologue to an unknown yet exciting future.

Jesus challenged them, "As I said before on this mountain, be perfect, therefore, as your heavenly Father is perfect."

The people stole glances at each other—even if they faithfully obeyed and did their best, was it possible to be perfect?

"I know this is a hard saying. When I tell you to be perfect, it's a command—a challenge to be a little more like me each day, as my brothers and sisters. My Father and I know that, at times, you'll fail. Yet, the same phrase is also a promise. My Father, who has begun a good work in you, will continue to mold and strengthen you, till you are complete and mature.

"And so eventually, through God's grace and refining, you *will* be perfect."

Reflect

1. There are varying interpretations of how literally people should take the Sermon on the Mount, from 100 percent literal to mostly idealistic or symbolic. How much of it do you think Jesus really meant us to obey?
2. Where do you see signs of progress in your life of God making you perfect and completing his work in you? Where do you think he still needs to work?

Learn

In 1 Corinthians 15:6, Paul lists many of those to whom Jesus appeared after his resurrection. Questions are raised in particular about the five hundred mentioned here: who they were, exactly when did Jesus appear to them, and what did he say? Near the western shore of the Sea, just across the Via Maris, is Mount Eremos, traditionally considered the site of the Sermon on the Mount. Near the foot of that mountain is the Cave of Eremos (mentioned earlier with the Sons of Thunder), which has been there since before Jesus' time. On top of that cave today is a rock about five feet high, with a cross like a plus, five Cs (Roman numerals for 500), and eleven marks, one for each apostle—all of which suggest this may mark the spot where Jesus appeared to the five hundred. While no one can be sure, it is a possible or even likely spot for this event.

Vignette 43
I Give You My Mind and My Spirit

Matthew 13:17; 1 Peter 1:10-12; Isaiah 40:10-14;
1 Corinthians 2:6-15

Saturday morning, people gathered once again in the synagogue to worship and to learn more about the new kingdom. There was not an empty place to be found—the crowd again overflowed the building. By now, most people in Capernaum had put their faith in Jesus. Those who were still uncertain about Jesus' identity or rejected him outright were a dwindling group. The same was true for many of the smaller villages around, like Chorazin, Magdala, and Bethsaida. Though they had been slow to believe, now they were convinced.

With Jesus' teaching about the kingdom and the coming group of believers called the church, the Jews accepted that their way of worship would change. But still, many were confused about what would happen to old traditions and practices. Would they all be discarded or changed dramatically? What new requirements would this kingdom bring? Would the new church replace the synagogue?

Jesus was aware of their questions and doubts. He began, "I

know that these changes are unsettling, and many of you are uneasy." His eyes probed faces in every corner of the synagogue. "Some of what comes will be totally new. Yet everything my Father and I are doing has been planned from long ago, even before creation itself, and builds on what He has done throughout our history. What's happening now is the culmination of his plan. Many wished to see what you now see, but they died before it happened.

"Do you remember what Isaiah said about my Father?" Jesus asked. "'*See, the Sovereign Lord comes with power, and he rules with a mighty arm'... He tends his flock like a shepherd: he gathers the lambs in his arms and carries them close to his heart.'*[1]... '*Since ancient times no one has heard, no ear has perceived, no eye has seen any God besides you, who acts on behalf of those who wait for him. You come to the help of those who gladly do right, who remember your ways.'*"[2]

The people nodded as they recalled these well-known verses and how they had seen God's character and work throughout history.

Jesus sought to plant his next words deep in their hearts. "Some of my ideas have been difficult to accept—but these ideas are the core of the new Kingdom, and how it must function." He measured carefully his next words, as if precisely laying stones for the foundation of a new Temple.

"My Father has now granted all power and authority to me, to rule and provide in every way just as he did. I am the center of a new fellowship. I am the channel through which all blessings, strength, and guidance will be passed on to you. I am the good shepherd who will seek and save the lost, and care for the flock—no one can snatch my sheep out of my hand. My Father and I are one. Our work is one, our goals are one. And now you all will be one with me.

"Now my Father is doing a new thing. Isaiah asked, '*Who can fathom the Spirit of the Lord?*'[3] In Isaiah's time, the answer was that *no*

---

1. Isaiah 40:10-11 (NIV)
2. Isaiah 64:4-5 (NIV)
3. Isaiah 40:13 (NIV)

one could fully understand the Lord. It was unthinkable, absurd, impossible. Yet, I tell you that the Spirit of the Lord now lives in me, and what was once impossible for others will be possible for you."

The people exchanged puzzled glances, whispering quietly. With the air of one revealing a great privilege, Jesus stated simply, "To those who believe in me, who are part of my new church, I will give ... my mind."

The people heard but didn't understand. They held their breath, waiting for his next words.

Jesus explained, "Only a person's spirit knows the innermost thoughts of that person. In the same way, no one knows the thoughts of God except the Spirit of God. I'll give you the Spirit of God, and he will live in you as he lives in me. He'll make known to you what he receives from me, revealing God's thoughts, wisdom, and knowledge as you have need.

"And so, you will have my mind and my Spirit in you."

The people struggled to assimilate this stunning concept.

Jesus added, "I'll be connected to my disciples, my church, as the head is connected to the body. You'll have life as long as you're connected to me. Just as I did, you'll minister in different ways, with the gifts the Spirit and I will choose to grant each of you. And to you, I grant my power and authority.

"Therefore, if my Body has my mind and my Spirit, it should act just as I do. When this happens, I will still be able to live and minister on earth through your hearts and words and deeds!'"

Reflect

1. How does this brief story complement what Jesus says about the Spirit in John 14-16?
2. How could your life and actions be different if Jesus' mind and spirit are acting *through* you instead of just being *with* you when you are doing things?

Learn

For a description of synagogue history, worship, practices, uses, and design, as well as a summary of biblical stories occurring in synagogues, see the video of Class 8 from this Life of Christ course: https://ibitibi.org/en/life-of-christ

Vignette 44

You Will Drink the Cup I Drink

Matthew 24:4-51, 16:21-27, 10:5-42; Ephesians 6:10-18;
Mark 16:17-18

Jesus and the disciples were now on the second day of their four-day journey back to Jerusalem. As they walked early Monday morning, Thomas asked Jesus, "Lord, why did we take this road through Samaria instead of the way along the Jordan, like we usually do?"

Jesus, the rabbi, evaluated the question, capitalizing on an opportunity to teach more than had been asked. "Thomas, do you remember on the mountain in Galilee, when I said there are two ways people may take?"

"I think so," replied Thomas. "You said the narrow way led to life, and the broad way led to death."

"Correct," said Jesus. "Even though there are several roads to Jerusalem, the goal of the trip usually determines which road we choose. I know this road is possibly more dangerous and more difficult to walk, and it's certainly one most Jews avoid. Yet, during this trip, I want to visit some important people who live along this way. They justify the extra effort and danger that we will face.

"What I do, and what each of my followers will need to do, is choose actions based not on personal comfort or profit, convenience, or safety, but rather on what will best achieve the will of our Father and his Kingdom. To do otherwise eventually leads to serving Satan and his kingdom.

"I need you all to assess your ministry from now on in light of this spiritual conflict—who influences you, where you go, what activities you undertake, how you teach others. From now on, everything you are, have, and do must be put at the service of the kingdom. The consequences will be costly and difficult. Not everyone will like or agree with what you do. They may try to persuade you to take a different way. But your spiritual goals should always dictate your path."

The disciples listened intently, edging closer to Jesus as they walked.

"Many groups make up Israel—Jews, Gentiles, Samaritans, Romans, Zealots, Herodians, and more." He glanced at several of them as he named the groups from which they came. "Each one has a particular objective or perspective that is most important to them —political power, Torah, money, freedom, justice—and that objective dictates their actions.

"You know this because some of your arguments these last three years have been about these very things. But now you must lay all arguments aside to focus on the spiritual battle between God and Satan, good and evil, truth and falsehood, my Father's kingdom and the Accuser's kingdom.

"What do you remember from our conversation the day that we left the Temple and sat on the Mount of Olives to talk about the signs of the end?"

Andrew said, "You said that false teachers, false prophets, and even false Christs would arise and would try to deceive many—even the elect."

Philip added, "That many people would turn away from the truth to betray and hate each other."

Nathanael offered, "And that we should expect wars, famines, and earthquakes, nations, and kingdoms set against each other."

"Exactly!" Jesus exclaimed. "All those things are only symptoms of the deeper struggle that has gone on since the beginning of creation. No matter the place, people, issues, or events, all grow out of the roots of the spiritual battle between God and Satan.

"Since the root of the problem is spiritual, then the answer must also be spiritual. Physical weapons can't conquer a spiritual enemy. Money can't cover a spiritual deficit. Power can't force obedience to a spiritual master. Earthly governments can't eliminate demonic forces through laws or politics.

"Only spiritual weapons will be effective and triumph: truth, God's righteousness, the gospel of peace, love, faith, salvation, grace, the word of God, the Spirit of God, and prayer.

Turning to Peter, he reminded him, "This is why, at Caesarea Philippi, I told you that my suffering, death, and resurrection were the only way to defeat sin, idolatry, and rebellion.

The group slowed to a halt and gathered around Jesus. They were beginning to understand. Many times in the last three years, they had seen compassion, kindness, and service conquer hatred, selfishness, and meanness.

Jesus spoke with quiet intensity. "This is also why I said that you will drink the cup I drink and be baptized with my baptism." He reflected a moment and said solemnly, "Most of you will even give your lives for others."

They recalled other words of Jesus which now seemed more urgent and real:

"I'm sending you out like sheep among wolves."

"All men will hate you because of me..."

"Brother will betray brother to death..."

"A man's enemies will be the members of his own household."

"When you are persecuted in one place, flee to another."

"I did not come to bring peace, but a sword."

"When they arrest you …"

"Be on your guard against men. They will hand you over to the local councils and flog you in their synagogues."

"Do not be afraid of those who can kill the body."

"Anyone who does not take his cross and follow me is not worthy of me."

"Whoever finds his life will lose it, and whoever loses his life for my sake will find it."

Even though they had seen Jesus confront opposition, persecution, and death, and even though they had suffered some with him, they had not fully understood. Now that they considered these warnings together, they realized that their new lives would be characterized more by suffering than comfort, more by sacrifice than gain, more by humble submission than positions of power.

They were sobered, uncertain. And they were afraid—not just of pain and loss, but that they would not measure up to the challenge. Peter fixed his eyes on the ground. He had already failed Jesus miserably and publicly. Would he crumble every time he faced danger?

Jesus read their hearts as they recalled his teachings and suffering and confronted the probability that they also would lose their lives if they followed him.

Finally, Jesus said gently, "Yes, I did say 'when' you are persecuted, not 'if.' I'm telling you now that you *will* suffer, and many of you *will* die for me." His words crashed down on them, and he saw more questions arise in their minds.

When will I die? Perhaps later this week in Jerusalem?

How will I die? Will I be crucified or stoned or beheaded?

Will I be put in jail like John or tortured and suffer for a long time? Will I break under the pressure and deny Jesus?

What will my family say? My wife? Maybe they won't want me to follow Jesus anymore …

They were miserable and confused. Somehow, these things had never seemed as real or as menacingly close as at this moment.

Jesus understood and spoke with deep compassion, "I didn't speak this plainly to you before because you couldn't bear it then. You had not yet seen my final suffering nor my impossible triumph.

"Once again—this is a spiritual battle that has been raging since creation. Now you will play your part." He paused, then spoke emphatically, "Because my Father and I have given you this task, we also will equip you in every way to do it.

"We'll give you the words to say in any situation you may confront, whether with the smallest child or the most powerful ruler. We'll give you all authority to teach and bind and overcome the power of the enemy. We'll give you power to heal, raise the dead, drive out demons, cleanse lepers, and speak in tongues. For the rest of your lives, you'll be able to do whatever my Father shows you to do.

"Even if you suffer and die, I'll be with you each moment to strengthen you and give you whatever you lack. Afterward, my Father will take you into glory, where there will be no more death or mourning or crying or pain. He will wipe every tear from your eyes. Be faithful, even to the point of death, and I will give you the crown of life."

Jesus examined their faces, then moved through the group—grasping a shoulder, giving a hug, looking deeply into their eyes as he communicated his understanding, support, and love for each one. Then slowly he turned south again, and gesturing with his head, summoning them to resume the journey.

As the group slowly spread out behind him, in single file or in pairs, Thomas murmured to Matthew, "I was just asking why we took this road!"

Reflect

1. Look at the spiritual armor described in Ephesians 6:10-18. How is each part of the armor in some way connected to Jesus?
2. Have you had to suffer for Jesus? If so, in what way?
3. In what ways are seeking comfort and self-gratification the most dangerous obstacles to following Jesus?

Learn

How did the apostles die? This four-minute video give some ideas, according to tradition.

https://www.gotquestions.org/apostles-die.html

Vignette 45

The Testimony of the Risen Saints

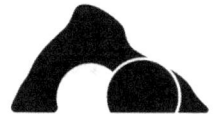

Genesis 14:17-20; Isaiah 61:10; Numbers 6:24-26

Wednesday morning was fresh and beautiful, and the miles passed quickly. It was almost noon when Jesus and his followers finally approached Jerusalem from the north, arriving in Bethany at the hospitable home of Mary, Martha, and Lazarus. After a long, relaxed lunch, during which each shared the experiences of the last three weeks, the group spent the afternoon resting from the journey.

As the sun set, the disciples gathered again. Then, people trickled into the house from Jerusalem. Mary, Martha, Lazarus, and Jesus greeted them as family. Jesus said to the disciples, "I want you to meet some old friends of mine—some of them very old!"

Jesus smiled at Matthew and Thomas. "Do you recognize anyone here?" Matthew saw one couple and exclaimed, "You're the ones we saw the day of the resurrection! But—you said that you'd come back to life, and that you were from the time of Hezekiah!"

Jesus nodded and gestured to the group. "The afternoon I died, my Father chose to raise these people to life again, and they went into the city on the day of my resurrection. You were some of the first people to see them, and you didn't believe them. But of course, they had a hard time believing it themselves!"

Jesus continued, "All these are servants of my Father from different eras of our history. Together, they represent God's people since the time of Abraham. They were present for key events in Israel's history and heard the promises which my Father made. Throughout the centuries, various ones had heard the prophets predict the coming of the Messiah. Then a few weeks ago, they met the Messiah himself!

"A few days after my resurrection, I met with them and gave them a mission—to go to Jerusalem and the villages around it every day and share their stories. They didn't only recount ancient events, they were also able to connect these events with the story of the Messiah. Tonight, we have the privilege of hearing what happened this month."

Jesus looked at them expectantly and invited, "Tell us your stories!"

After a brief silence, one man began, "I was a servant of Abraham for many years. I was with him when he first came into Canaan. Through the years, I gradually learned about God's promises to him and waited decades with him for them to be fulfilled.

"When Lot was taken with the prisoners of Sodom, I helped fight to recover the prisoners and goods that were lost. On the way home, we stopped again near Mount Moriah, and a man named Melchizedek came out to meet us.

"Melchizedek brought bread and wine to share with Abraham and blessed him. At that time, Abraham had received the promises from God but had not yet confirmed part of his covenant with God. In a sense, God met with Abraham that day *through* Melchizedek!

"Of course, I died without knowing about the law or the prophets, and only a little of how God would fulfill his promise about blessing the nations through Abraham. I've learned more this month than in my whole life with Abraham. Every night my friends have taught me about our people's history and the prophecies of the Messiah.

"My friends said that in the meeting with Melchizedek, God previewed who the Messiah would be and what roles he would play. Melchizedek was the king of Salem. His name means 'king of righteousness,' and Salem means 'peace.' He was also considered a priest of God. As the father of our nation, from Abraham would come all those whom Melchizedek represented—the house of David and of Aaron, the king and the priest.

"So, when Jesus came, all the promises God made were fulfilled in him. He is the King of Righteousness, the King of Peace, and the High Priest. This Son of David once again combines the kingship and the priesthood—the priestly king and the royal priest.

"As Jesus fulfilled God's covenant with Abraham, he gave his disciples a sign of the new covenant—bread and wine—the same elements which Melchizedek shared that day with Abraham. In a way, it's as if Melchizedek had returned to give again this blessing to the people of God.

"I was also with Abraham on the trip to Mount Moriah. Though he didn't take me up the mountain with him that day, Isaac told me later what happened, and how the Lord had provided a ram that day so he didn't die." He smiled faintly. "When Sarah found out what Abraham had done, she wasn't very happy about it!

"When God spared Abraham from sacrificing Isaac and provided a different sacrifice, it again foreshadowed what God would do later. That time, God did not spare his own son but sacrificed him for all of us—on the same mountain as where Abraham had been."

The disciples were fascinated to hear a first-hand account from someone who had witnessed some of the most famous events of their history and to understand how those events were connected to Jesus.

Next, a woman spoke up, "My husband and I were teenagers, not married yet, when Moses sent spies to scout out the promised land. When our parents and the others didn't believe that God could give us the land, we spent the next thirty-nine years wandering in the desert, wishing they had trusted more in God.

"Those desert years shaped our identity as a people. For us, the word 'desert' means a place of speaking—and indeed, we began to hear the words of God more clearly during those long, hard years. The desert was a holy sanctuary where we met with God and came to know him better.

"In the desert, we experienced God's care for us, as a shepherd cares for the flock. Our clothes didn't wear out. Every day we ate bread from heaven. He miraculously provided quail from over the sea and water from a rock." She chuckled. "A rock! Most people would think of rocks as obstacles, but God used rocks to give us water and shade. So even the rocks reminded us of him.

"When God raised us to life last month, we had to catch up on our history. As others told us stories of what Jesus had done during the last three years, we saw yet another example of God's faithfulness and provision through him—only this time, the provision was eternal.

"Our physical experiences in the desert helped us see clearly how God foreshadowed Jesus' identity and actions. He's the true manna from heaven, which gives life forever, not just a day. He's the living water from God the Rock, which quenches thirst forever. He's the living Stone, who is now also Bread. He clothes us with 'garments of salvation and arrays us in robes of righteousness.' He is God the shepherd, who came physically to care for us in the desert of life."

The disciples clearly remembered the day Jesus had fed the 5000, the discussion afterward with the Jews about bread from heaven, and how that teaching had driven off many followers. Yet now, hearing first-hand testimony from those who had experienced the desert wanderings, the disciples marveled, recognizing a different perspective on Jesus' message.

Another couple chimed in, "We were part of the first group of exiles to return from Babylonia to Jerusalem. As we approached the city, we saw that almost all the villages were deserted. The fields had

After the Tomb

lain fallow for seventy years and were totally overgrown, just as Jeremiah had prophesied.

"We walked among the ruins of Jerusalem in a daze. Nothing remained of the splendid Temple of Solomon, and the Temple Mount was deserted. Hardly any buildings in the city were still standing, and because the walls were destroyed, the city was in constant danger from vandals and thieves. Wild animals darted through the rubble and the bushes.

"Our grandparents were only ten years old when Nebuchadnezzar laid siege to the city. They remembered and recounted stories about the Temple, the gold, the beautiful craftsmanship, the Temple rituals and worship, and especially the annual feasts.

"Zerubbabel and Jeshua organized the exiles, and we began to rebuild the altar, then the Temple. We'll never forget the day when we finally finished laying the foundation of the Temple. With their trumpets and cymbals, the priests and the Levites led the people in praise, singing about the Lord's goodness.

"It was strange because we remembered those stories about the splendor of the Temple—and this Temple was hardly like it. Some of the older people who had come back with us wept, remembering the destruction of that former glory. Others felt only the joy of the new beginning and the confirmation that God had not forgotten us nor his promises.

"Since the Lord raised us from the dead a month ago, we've seen the same second Temple we built five hundred years ago—yet not the same, after Herod enlarged the Temple Mount and embellished the Temple.

"One day, we met a young priest in the Court of Prayer. He said one of his favorite jobs was to help light the four huge menorahs that stood in that Court during the feasts of Passover, Pentecost, and Tabernacles. He and the other young priests would take enormous wicks made from old priestly garments, and huge jars of oil, and climb fifty cubits to the top of the ladder, where they would fill with oil the four golden basins at the top of each menorah. When all the menorahs were lit, people said there was not a courtyard in Jerusalem that was not illuminated by them.

"During the feast of Tabernacles, the year before Jesus died, the young priest told us that a priest was performing the ceremony for the drawing of the water, and Jesus and his disciples were also worshiping there. The priests had just brought the water in the golden jar back from the Pool of Siloam and entered the Temple courts.

"Suddenly Jesus cried out, 'If anyone is thirsty, let him come to me and drink! Whoever believes in me, streams of living water will flow from within him!'

"No one knew what to do! The priests were angry at Jesus for interrupting because the people paid more attention to him than the ceremony. Before the priests could decide what to do, Jesus walked out of the Temple.

"The next day, Jesus came back to the Temple courts. The four great menorahs were again blazing away, and the people were worshiping in the Court of Prayer. Then Jesus pointed at the menorahs and announced to the people, 'I am the Light of the world! Whoever follows me will never walk in darkness but will have the Light of life.'

"And of course, the Pharisees were furious with him and challenged him to provide witnesses that his words were true.

"But the people murmured. They remembered what the rabbis had taught about the lighting of the Hanukkiah—the menorah they used for the Feast of Dedication. Each year at Hanukkah, a rabbi would bring the candle called the servant light from a synagogue and would light the candles of the Hanukkiah day by day.

"If Jesus said he was the Light of the world, could it be that God had sent this Light from heaven? And could he be the servant light that lights all the other lights? They connected these ideas from their history to Jesus' words, and many put their faith in him.

"My husband and I realized that we've seen prophecies fulfilled

After the Tomb

before our very eyes! Our grandparents had seen the original Temple, and years later, we helped rebuild it. Now we've seen Herod's Temple, and Jesus, who will build a Temple of living Stones from those who believe in him. We marveled at the splendor of the ceremonies of light and water in the Temple, and now we believe that Jesus is the Living Water and the Eternal Light."

The stories continued until the disciples were overwhelmed by these living testimonies from every era of Israel's history—and how every story or prophecy pointed in some way to Jesus.

The gathering ended long after midnight. After everyone else had gone to prepare to sleep, Jesus invited the group of risen servants to follow him. Leaving the house, he led them along a path, stopping at a ridge of the Mount of Olives. A soft breeze touched their faces as they stood silently, looking across the Kidron Valley to the sleeping city. Their faces glowed softly, the moonlight reflecting in their eyes. Suddenly everything was still, and the sounds of the night faded away.

Jesus commended them, "Well done, good and faithful servants! You were obedient to my Father not only in your first lives, but also in your short second lives this month. My Father and I are pleased with you. Enter into your reward! This time, you will remain in my Father's house forever. He will bless you and keep you, make his face shine upon you and be gracious to you, turn his face toward you and give you peace ... beginning *now*!"

And with those words, suddenly light flashed all around the group. The servants' faces shone brilliantly, and they were overcome with awe. The light seemed to divide into two enormous hands, which gently gathered them up, carrying them smoothly and effortlessly into the sky.

Reflect

1. What person from biblical history would you like to talk with, to hear their story? If you could go back to a certain place, or see a certain event, what would it be?
2. Each Christian continues the long story of God's relationship with his people. What stories could you tell from how God has worked in your life?

Learn

Consider these background passages to the risen saints' testimonies.

1. Abraham and Mount Moriah, Gen. 22
2. The rescue of Lot, Gen. 14
3. God did not spare his son, Rom. 8:32
4. He is our peace, Eph. 2:14
5. Bread and wine, Matt. 26:26ff
6. Moses sending out spies, Num. 13
7. Manna and quail, Ex. 16
8. Water from the rock, Ex. 17, Num. 20
9. Concepts of midbar, and all the Hebrew words connected to it. Strong's concordance (words #4057, 1696-99); related concepts from Ray Vander Laan's teaching on desert and *midbar* in his Faith Lessons, DVD #12 about the desert.
10. Jesus is true bread from heaven, John 6:32, 41, 50, 51
11. Jesus as living Stone, who is also bread, 1 Pet. 2:4, Matt. 4:3
12. Jesus is living water, John 4:14, 7:37
13. Jesus as shepherd, John 10, 1 Pet. 5:4
14. 70 years in exile, Jer. 25:10, 29:10
15. Rebuilding of altar and temple, Ezra 3.

16. Great menoroth in Court of Prayer, Mishnah in Sukkkot 5:2-3, Garrard p. 66, https://www.sefaria.org/Mishnah_Sukkah.5.6?lang=bi
17. Jesus inviting people to come to him and drink, John 7:37
18. Jesus the light of the world, John 8:12ff
19. Many put their faith in him. John 8:30

Vignette 46
We Were Blind, But Now We See

John 9

The merchants' street of the Tyropoeon Valley in Jerusalem slowly came to life on Friday morning as the sun rose over the eastern wall of the Temple courts. Rafael helped his parents open their small cheesemaking shop, setting out trays on the shelves near the street.

Rafael wrapped a block of cheese and handed it to a woman, then turned to the next customer. He was stunned and delighted—it was the man who had healed him! Rafael called out. "Mother! Come quickly! Jesus is here!" She emerged from the back of the shop, wiping her hands on a towel.

Seeing Jesus took her back to the day when Rafael had walked into their shop and seen his parents for the first time in his life!

At first, she thought he was home early from begging in the Temple, but when he came close and hugged her and his father, she realized his eyes could see everything! Joy clashed with confusion. She wanted to ask him about everything, but then she saw the crowd following Rafael down the street—neighbors, friends, customers, and in the back, stalking angrily toward them, some of the chief Pharisees!

One of them thrust his way to the front of the crowd and brusquely confronted them. "Is this your son?" he asked.

"Yes ..." the father faltered, his joy sliding into the beginnings of fear. What had Rafael done? Why was this man angry with them?

"Was he born blind?" the man demanded.

"Yes ..."

"Then how was he healed?" the Pharisee barked.

"We know he is our son," ventured the mother. "But how he can see now or who opened his eyes, we don't know."

The Pharisee seethed in silence, waiting for a more complete answer. The mother and father, stampeded by the attack, suddenly wondered if Rafael had done something that might cause them to lose their place in the synagogue and community.

They stammered, "Ask him. He is of age. He can speak for himself."

The rest of the conversation hadn't gone well. Rafael had insisted on defending Jesus as a man of God and a prophet, defying and humiliating the Pharisees in front of everyone. Furious, unable to counter Rafael's arguments, they had insulted him and thrown him out of the synagogue.

Now, the man who had healed their son was standing in their shop. "Quite a bit different today than that day, isn't it?" remarked Jesus, seemingly unperturbed by the memories flooding her mind.

She decided to answer him honestly. "My husband and I were ashamed later when the crowds finally left. Our son had been healed and had stood up to the Pharisees and defended you—and we were more worried about our status in the synagogue!"

The father chimed in. "When we ate supper that night with Rafael, he told us the whole story—how you had treated him with compassion and not judged him as others had, and how he had been healed. Rafael was kind to us—kinder than we deserved," he admitted.

"That Sabbath, we went to the synagogue—without Rafael, of course. The rabbi had been told to ask us what we believed about who you were. We said we didn't know for certain, but that you seemed to teach the Word of God and have the power of God, and we believed in you.

"The rabbi was furious. He couldn't believe it. 'Consider your answer well! If you believe in this man Jesus, you have no place here! Is that what you want?'

"We were shaking, but we had told Rafael that we believed him—and no one could deny the miracle! So, we told him yes, and he threw us out too.

"Where could we go? We left the synagogue and went to the Temple. There, we found Rafael with a group of people who said they had followed you to Jerusalem from Galilee. They gave us the same welcome they had given to Rafael earlier. Since that day, we've met with them each Sabbath and kept up with the news about you."

The woman added, "When we heard you'd been killed, we were devastated. Then we heard the rumors of your resurrection. Yet, since we didn't see you, we wavered between hope and uncertainty. Now you're here—alive!"

Rafael and his parents knelt before Jesus there in the street. Those passing by looked at them curiously. "Please tell us, Jesus. What do we do now? How can we thank you for healing our son and changing our lives?"

Jesus touched them gently and gestured for them to stand. "Thank you for believing in me, even though it cost you your fellowship in the synagogue and hurt your business. You've been faithful to me and testified about me to many. My Father has seen this, and he will reward you.

"I give you three a special task now. Rafael, you know that your name means 'healed of God.' I healed your eyes with mud! All of you are convinced that I am of God. Who better than you three can testify to the blind about who I am and what I've done for you? So, I'm sending you to seek out the blind people in Israel, to share your story with them. Little by little, year by year, you can help many move from shadows to light, from despair to hope.

"As your first step, I'm sending you to meet a man named Bartimaeus in Jericho and another named Seth in Bethsaida. Your family and theirs have much in common."

Then Jesus reached out and took their hands in his, eight hands locked together. He said, "I grant you the power to heal the blind whom you'll meet in the coming years. At the same time, I grant you the knowledge and authority to teach about spiritual blindness, and to show people the way out of that darkness as well. I commission you to share this power and authority with Bartimaus and Seth. Between you all, you'll carry on my ministry of healing the blind after I return to my Father in heaven.

Jesus smiled sadly. "Not everyone will be pleased. Some will be jealous. Some will accuse you of healing by the power of the devil and question your motives. They said the same to me." He looked deep into their eyes. "Will you do this?"

"We will!" they promised.

Jesus held their gaze a moment, then smiled. "I know you will. And remember I will be with you ... always."

Reflect

1. Compare the reaction of Jesus to the blind man in John 9 and the paralytic in John 5. What role might sin play in the things that cause us suffering—or not?
2. The blind man was not healed immediately. He had to walk about a half-mile to the Pool of Siloam. Can you think of a time when Jesus' answer to your need required steps of faith and obedience before you got what you needed?

Learn

A man from England named Alec Garrard spent 33,000 hours over 30 years building a model of Herod's Temple Mount in his backyard. He baked every tile and brick, made and painted 4000 figures historically correct costumes to put around the model. Many scholars consider it to be the most accurate representation of the Temple available. Then he wrote a book describing the Temple itself and the courts in great detail, as well as its practices in Jewish life, feasts, and sacrifices. It is an extremely useful tool, called *The Splendor of the Temple*, from Grand Rapids: Kregel Publications, 2000.

Vignette 47

He Stopped Sinning, and Something Better Happened to Him

John 5:1-15

Rimon was back where he had spent more time than any other place in his life—the pool of Bethesda. Thirty-eight long years lying paralyzed on a mat—waiting, hoping, daily trying to fight his way to the pool so that somehow an angel might heal him.

Many had been there for years, but Rimon was the veteran, who had suffered longer than anyone else. As younger, less crippled people beat him to the water day by day, seemingly healed, his bitterness intensified, and his hope dwindled.

Then Jesus had come. Out of all the people at the pool, this stranger had chosen to speak to him, then heal him. Months later, the healing and the conversations with Jesus seemed slightly unreal. For days, he pondered the words Jesus said to him at their second encounter, "Stop sinning, or something worse may happen to you!" Jesus added nothing else. What did he know about Rimon's life?

After Jesus healed him, Rimon felt drawn to the pool again. He brought the invalids food, water, clothing, or something to shade them from the sun. If they asked—or even if they didn't ask—he would tell them the story of Jesus. Eventually, they always asked, "But what did Jesus *do*? And what words did he use?" As if they, too, would be freed if they could just capture the magic formula.

Sometimes, they muttered more poignant questions: "If he healed *you* that day, why not *me*? Wasn't I worthy or important enough? Didn't he care about me or have time for me?"

Rimon would say simply, "I don't know. I didn't think I was worthy or important, but for some reason, he healed me." And he would urge them, "If Jesus comes back, ask him to heal you."

On this day, Rimon was chatting with a friend over a simple meal. As he glanced around, his gaze paused on a man who had just entered the building, walking purposefully toward them. He jumped to his feet and squinted. Could it be? Yes!

"Jesus!" he cried out. "Come over here!"

"I'm coming," Jesus called in return with a smile. Soon, he was sitting on the ground by them, talking to Rimon and his friend, whose eyes were wide with wonder ... and hope.

As Jesus conversed with them, he asked the man, "Friend, what do you want me to do for you?"

Gathering his courage, the man said, "I just want to be healed—to go back to my family and a normal life. Can you help me?"

So, Jesus healed him.

Then Rimon led Jesus from friend to friend. Jesus greeted them, listened to their stories, laid hands on them in blessing, and healed them all. Within two hours, the pool of Bethesda was deserted and silent, but the streets outside were filled with men and women and children laughing and jumping and running home to their families and friends, shouting their news to anyone who would listen.

Jesus and Rimon stood at the entrance to the pool, watching them go. Then Jesus turned to Rimon and asked him gently, "Do you have another question for me, Rimon?"

Had Jesus read his mind? But of course! If Jesus could heal his body and heart, he could also know his mind. Suddenly Rimon felt relieved, free to ask what had been troubling him. "I do," he admitted. "When you told me that day to stop sinning, or something worse could happen, did you mean that something I had done had caused my suffering for those long years?"

Jesus was silent for a moment, then fixed a piercing gaze on him. "Tell me, Rimon, what was your family life like before you were hurt?"

Rimon felt ashamed and embarrassed. Did Jesus already know what had happened? He hesitated a long time before answering, then confessed in a low voice.

"In my family, I was *not* a good husband or father. My parents arranged a marriage with a woman in our village, but because she wasn't the one I wanted, I wasn't happy with her. We lived together, and to outsiders we were a normal couple. At home, she tried to be a good wife, but nothing could satisfy me. I found fault with anything she did, and the arguments would begin. Night after night, we'd fight, and I'd leave the house, sometimes to drink. When I'd return, she'd already be asleep, or pretending to be.

"Yet we conceived somehow, and she gave me a daughter. That helped for a while; I tried to be a better husband and father. But as the years passed, I went back to my old ways. My wife became bitter and resentful, cold and angry. So, I used that to justify more time away from her, more drinking.

"Our daughter grew up seeing this. My actions distanced her from me. She was confused, frightened, and increasingly unhappy. As she grew up, she responded to me with bitterness and coldness, as my wife did. I knew they didn't love or respect me. They were happier when I wasn't there.

"It wasn't right, and I'm not proud of it, but I decided that if my own wife and daughter rejected me, then I would seek happiness elsewhere. So, I found a woman on the outskirts of Jerusalem and began to visit her several nights a month.

"My wife and daughter suspected. Finally, one night they caught me when I was coming home from the woman's house, and they confronted me. I'd already drunk too much that night. I was embarrassed to be caught and furious with them because I felt as if they'd driven me to it." Rimon stopped here, and tears came into his eyes.

"We began to argue and scream at each other. I lost control and started to hit my wife in the face and the stomach, and she was hitting me too. Our daughter rushed in to stop us, but I lashed out and hit her too. She fell to the floor, stunned.

"When my wife saw that, she shrieked and jumped on me, pounding me with her fists, pushing me toward the door, yelling, 'Get out! Get out! I never want to see you again!'"

"I stumbled out the door and into the street. Just then a wagon loaded with heavy stones was passing by. I fell directly in front of it. The driver tried to stop, but it was too late. It ran over me, crushed my legs, and broke my back."

Rimon stopped, breathing heavily, tears flowing down his face, locked into the memory of that awful night. Jesus sighed and put an arm around his shoulders but remained quiet.

Finally, Rimon continued, "For the next thirty-eight years, I had no home or family. I rarely saw my wife and daughter, and then only at a distance. Our friends sided with her, and I don't blame them.

"I lay there daily by the pool, alternating between hoping for healing and longing for death. When you healed me that day, you restored part of my life—but where could I go? My wife wouldn't take me back. I didn't even know where my daughter had gone. I heard she'd taken up with some questionable people, but then, who was I to judge her?

"Since you healed me, I've worked at simple jobs around Jerusalem and told people here about you. But all the while, I've wondered if somehow I could regain my family."

Jesus said, "Thank you for telling me your story. I can see that you took it to heart when I told you to stop sinning. You've changed more than you realize, but I know that it's been difficult for you.

"In a way, your sins with your family *did* cause you to be injured, especially what you did that night. But when I healed you, I also forgave you. Now you are free to forgive others, and they might forgive you. Think about what you could do with that opportunity—even with your wife and daughter."

Reflect

1. How can we strike a balance between listening to others share problems with empathy, not judging them, and at the same time help them learn how to avoid or recover from harmful behaviors?
2. How do you deal with it when it seems like God ignores your prayers for a long time, even years?

Learn

The Israel Museum in Jerusalem has a model of Jerusalem in the time of Jesus, covering a quarter acre, at scale of 50:1 to real-life Jerusalem in the day. It is helpful for understanding the overall geography and major sections and buildings of first-century Jerusalem. John Delancey (of Biblical Israel Ministries) has a short, interesting video on it, with some wonderful drone footage starting about 3:10 in this video:

https://www.youtube.com/watch?v=HTFcqJraHOo

Vignette 48

New Life After Being Rescued

John 7:53-8:11

From the pool of Bethesda, Jesus walked southeast through the streets of Jerusalem, finally knocking on the door of a small house in the Lower City.

When a woman opened the door and saw Jesus, her face broke into a welcoming smile. "I'm so glad you came to see me! Since the morning you saved my life, I've kept up with what you were doing."

Jesus smiled and said, "I wanted to see how you've been, Miryam. Tell me about your life since that morning."

Miryam invited Jesus into her home. She took a minute to gather her thoughts, then replied slowly, yet willingly, "I thought that would be my last morning on earth. When the Pharisees burst into the room where I was sleeping with Hanan, I realized a trap had been set for me. If they had really wanted to punish adultery, they would've taken us both, but they let Hanan escape.

"Then they dragged me to the Temple and threw me on the pavement in front of you. Out of the corner of my eye, I saw them picking up rocks. They were certain you would have to let them stone me, and I knew I deserved it. I had surrendered all hope."

Jesus inwardly relived every moment with her.

"But you were wiser than they were, and you ruined their trap. After they drifted away, I was there with you, still certain I would be punished. I could hardly believe it when you showed me mercy instead of condemning me. I fled back to my house and cried for hours, overwhelmed by the day's emotions—anger, terror, and shame, but also relief and gratitude.

"After that day, I knew I should find different work, so I went to vendors all over Jerusalem, seeking any kind of job. But they refused me. The wives were afraid for me to be near their husbands, and the husbands despised what I had been, though some had been my clients.

"Finally, a couple and their son had mercy on me. Wait—you know them! Rafael and his parents. They knew what it was like to be rejected, so they offered me a small salary to help them occasionally in their shop."

Jesus nodded. "I'm so glad for you and them. I know you've all been a blessing to each other. I'm proud of your obedience to what I asked you to do, even though it was a difficult change.

"As I was drawing on the ground that day, my Father revealed your past to me. You were mistreated and unloved by your father, which led to years of fear, resentment, and bitterness. Even your name means 'rebellion,' an apt description. Since you left home at a young age, you've rebelled against every authority you saw—and paid the consequences."

Miryam lowered her eyes, convicted by Jesus' words because she knew they described her past exactly. Yet, even in her distress, she clung to hope. Jesus had been the first man in her life to show her compassion and set her on a new path. Perhaps he would guide her once again.

Jesus said gently, "As I told you then, I do *not* condemn you. Instead, I come to redeem you because my Father and I love you. We see great promise in you." He paused and let the silence stretch until she raised her eyes to his. His gaze was the same as it had been that previous morning—warm, accepting, reassuring ... life-giving!

Hot tears of relief and gratitude ran down her face, and she asked, "What can I do for you? How can I thank you?" She could not imagine how to repay his limitless mercy.

Jesus took her questions at face value. "There *is* a way you can show kindness, just as you have received it. I want you to go to the people you've hurt or deceived during these last years. Go to at least one person each day and ask if you can share your story with them. Then tell them you're sorry for how you've hurt them and ask for their forgiveness.

"Most will listen to you, whether from surprise or curiosity. Some will forgive you; others will not. Still others may curse you and throw you out. You'll be surprised how an apology can heal and how this simple act will open unexpected doors for you. My Father will bless you and others as you do this."

Miryam sat still, considering the challenge. She knew she should do it. She wanted to commit to it but was daunted by the enormous task, knowing that many could scorn or reject her. Yet none of her previous choices had brought her blessing—only enmity, loathing, and distress.

Jesus watched her face and prayed for his Father to give her the conviction and courage to obey. "Just one person at a time," he repeated.

She looked at him resolutely. She could trust this man with her life. He had already given it back to her once. A deeper life awaited with this new challenge.

"I'll do it!" she declared. "But who should I go to first?"

Jesus looked at her soberly for a moment. "You should begin with your father."

She caught her breath. She would not have chosen for him to be first. But she was determined, and so she nodded. "I'll do it first thing tomorrow morning," she promised.

"Do it tonight," Jesus urged her. "I just left him. You'll find him at the gate of the pool of Bethesda."

Reflect

1. What do you think Jesus wrote on the ground that morning of John 8? What made the Jewish leaders leave? And why did they leave starting with the oldest?
2. Max Lucado wrote about this story: "The Pharisees had the Word of God in their mouths, and rocks in their hands." How can we love and honor the Word of God, without turning it into a weapon to attack others?

Learn

Randy Alcorn's book, *The Grace and Truth Paradox*, is based on the words of John 1:14, "The Word became flesh and dwelt among us. We have seen his glory, the glory of the One and Only, who came from the Father, full of grace and truth." Alcorn says, "It's a two-point checklist of Christlikeness. Instead of the world's apathy and tolerance, we offer grace. Instead of the world's relativism and deception, we offer truth. If we minimize grace, the world sees no hope for salvation. If we minimize truth, the world sees no need for salvation."

VIGNETTE 49

FINAL WORDS, FINAL MIRACLE

Luke 24:50-52; Acts 1:6-11

It was Thursday morning, Jesus' final day on earth. The atmosphere at Lazarus' home was quiet, almost solemn, as if all sensed that something momentous was about to happen. After breakfast, Jesus and all the disciples set out toward the southern peak of the Mount of Olives, almost directly east of the Temple across the Kidron Valley.

Arriving at the summit, the group gathered around Jesus. For the last time on earth, he looked deeply into their eyes, loving them, empathizing with them, feeling their curiosity and uncertainty. They returned his gaze silently, remembering their own private moments with him over the last three years, beginning with the invitation to follow him to the bitterness of the crucifixion, the stunningly wonderful news of his resurrection, and the joyous, precious moments of the last forty days.

Simon the Zealot and Peter, side by side, remembered the Sunday seven weeks earlier when they had descended the Mount of Olives as part of a cheering multitude, waving palm branches, singing triumphant songs.

Simon knew that Jesus' methods were different from his. Yet, was it possible, since Jesus had accomplished the entire will of his Father, that he would declare his earthly kingdom today? A small spark of hope grew in him, and he timidly asked Jesus, "Lord, are you going to restore the kingdom to Israel at this time?"

Jesus turned his eyes on Simon, knowing his thoughts, but shook his head slowly. "It's not for you to know the times or dates the Father has set by his own authority."

Simon acknowledged Jesus' words, his hope short-lived.

"But you will all receive power when the Holy Spirit comes on you. And you will all be my witnesses in Jerusalem, and in all Judea and Samaria, and to the ends of the earth. Wait for the Spirit to come, and for my Father to show you what you should do. And remember all that I've told you during these last three years together."

Suddenly, they realized that he was saying goodbye. They pressed in closer to him. Those nearest him reached out to touch him once more—his shoulders, arms, hands—trying to hold on to him physically for these last few seconds.

Jesus smiled at all of them tenderly, perfect love shining from his eyes. He lifted his hands slowly, with all the others' hands still resting on him. He placed one on his mother Mary and the other on John. His gaze traveled slowly around the group.

Then he spoke a final blessing, well-known to them all, the priestly blessing from the eternal High Priest. "May my Father bless you and keep you; may his face shine upon you and may he be gracious to you; may he turn his face toward you and give you peace."

Then they noticed that his feet had left the ground. He was rising straight up! He was quickly beyond their reach and continued to ascend into the air toward heaven, and finally, a cloud hid him from their sight. They stood speechless. Once again, Jesus had done

After the Tomb

something none of them had ever seen before. Spellbound, they continued to gaze into the sky, wondering if he would reappear.

A sudden brightness shone near the disciples. They lowered their gaze from the heavens. Two men in white were smiling at them in amusement. Mary Magdalene and Joanna gasped. These were the same angels they had seen at the tomb!

"Galileans!" the men said, "why do you stand here looking at the sky?"

Peter answered, "We hoped Jesus might come back to us." He laughed in disbelief, adding, "And we've never seen anyone rise up into the sky before." A chuckle went through the group.

"Jesus won't come back to you at this time," the angels informed them. "He's gone into heaven now. Later on, he'll come back in the same way you saw him leave." Without answering questions, the angels vanished as suddenly as they had appeared.

As if waking from a dream, the group of disciples took a deep breath, trading disbelieving looks. Then they turned instinctively to Peter. He was silent for a moment, then said decisively, "Let's go back to Jerusalem and do what Jesus told us. We'll pray and study and talk together as we wait for the Spirit."

Slowly they made their way back to their house in the Essene Quarter, some conversing in low tones, others immersed in a jumble of thoughts and emotions. Jesus was gone, and no one knew when he would come back. They grieved for him, yet not as for one lost to death.

The Spirit was coming, and a new commission awaited them.

Reflect

1. The disciples didn't know when the Spirit would come, only that they must wait till he did. What do you think they did in the ten days between the ascension and Pentecost, besides selecting a replacement for Judas? (Acts 1)
2. How can you productively handle periods of waiting when you have no specific date or goal in sight for the next activity?

Learn

Matthew's account of the Great Commission in Galilee almost implies that Jesus spoke those words and then ascended. However, both accounts of the actual Ascension in Luke and Acts place it in Jerusalem on the Mount of Olives. No site has been confirmed as the exact spot, though there is an Ascension Edicule on the southern ridge of the Mount, in which supposedly on the floor is a framed "Rock of Ascension," containing the last earthly footprints of Jesus. Other locations suggested are the Russian Church of the Ascension, the Greek-Orthodox Monastery of the Ascension, and the Lutheran Church of the Ascension, part of the Augusta Victoria complex.

Another interesting detail is that ascension stories were fairly common in the time of Jesus, usually part of the deification of an important person, such as the traditions surrounding Augustus Caesar, Romulus (founder of Rome), or the Greek hero Heracles. In the case of Jesus, the Christians seemed to understand it as part of God vindicating Jesus after his death and confirming his eternal authority over all things.

Vignette 50

Pentecost in the Temple—the Church is Born

Acts 2:1-41; Leviticus 23:10; Exodus 20, 32; Ezekiel 1:4-24; 2 Corinthians 3:7-18

Pentecost! Fifty days since Passover weekend when Jesus had died. The group of 120 believers rose early to prepare to celebrate this feast day with thousands of their fellow Jews. Well before eight o'clock in the morning, pilgrims packed the streets, streaming toward the Temple courts from the city and all the roads leading into it. As was the custom, the worshipers approached the Temple from the south, cleansing themselves in the many purification baths before continuing up the Southern Steps and through the Double Gates to the Temple courts.

The group of 120 disciples eventually assembled in the Court of Prayer, since women were permitted to participate in the worship there. They mingled with the many friends and relatives who had come to Jerusalem for the feast, sharing smiles and hugs.

At 9 a.m., a priest blew the shofar from the southwest corner of the Temple, far above the courts, and the worship began with the typical readings of Pentecost, led by the priests. While listening,

Peter marveled at the throng of people that jammed the courts, as the reading from Exodus continued.

"... *On the morning of the third day there was thunder and lightning, with a thick cloud over the mountain, and a very loud trumpet blast. Everyone in the camp trembled. Then Moses led the people out of the camp to meet with God, and they stood at the foot of the mountain. Mount Sinai was covered with smoke, because the* Lord *descended on it in fire. The smoke billowed up from it like smoke from a furnace, the whole mountain trembled violently, and the sound of the trumpet grew louder and louder. Then Moses spoke and the voice of God answered him ...*"

Matthew remembered how the rabbis taught that at Mount Sinai, the thunder represented the voice of God, bringing the Law to the people, and that as the Lord's voice rang out, it was split into seventy different voices, each in a different language, so the whole world could understand the Law.

The priests moved on to the next readings. "*I looked, and I saw a windstorm coming out of the north—an immense cloud with flashing lightning and surrounded by brilliant light. The center of the fire looked like glowing metal, and in the fire was what looked like four living creatures ...*"[1]

These words resonated strongly within John, as if they were a melody he almost recognized, or had heard from a distance at some point in his life.

"... *Wherever the spirit would go, they would go, without turning as they went. The appearance of the living creatures was like burning coals of fire or like torches. Fire moved back and forth among the creatures; it was bright, and lightning flashed out of it.*"[2]

The multitude listened in rapt silence, as if the words were not describing events 600 years before, but rather something that was happening to them right then.

"... *When the living creatures moved, the wheels beside them moved;*

---

1. Ezekiel 1:4-5 (NIV)
2. Ezekiel 1:12-13 (NIV)

and when the living creatures rose from the ground, the wheels also rose. Wherever the spirit would go, they would go, and the wheels would rise along with them, because the spirit of the living creatures was in the wheels. When the creatures moved, they also moved; when the creatures stood still, they also stood still; and when the creatures rose from the ground, the wheels rose along with them, because the spirit of the living creatures was in the wheels.

"Spread out above the heads of the living creatures was what looked like an expanse, sparkling like ice, and awesome. Under the expanse their wings were stretched out one toward the other, and each had two wings covering its body. When the creatures moved, I heard the sound of their wings, like the roar of rushing waters, like the voice of the Almighty, like the tumult of an army."[3]

Jesus' mother Mary remembered nights when she would sit by Jesus as he went to sleep, sensing a host of invisible celestial beings, just beyond her sight, watching over her family.

The reading then described how the Lord commissioned Ezekiel to carry the word of God to the people. *"Son of man, go now to the house of Israel and speak my words to them."*[4]

Suddenly from everywhere in the Temple courts came the sound of a mighty rushing wind, filling the house of the Lord. People looked all around, above, and behind, toward the doors on all sides. Then, as if shooting out of the unseen wind, fire raced among them, separating into tongues.

The 120 disciples were mesmerized as if the stories of Sinai and Ezekiel were merging with this celebration today—the Spirit, the rushing wind, the fire—and they were in the center of it all! They saw the tongues come near them and hover exactly above their heads—only above the 120, no one else.

They felt the rushing wind buffet them, yet the flames still burned strong and bright. It seemed the wind enveloped them,

---

3. Ezekiel 1:19-24 (NIV)
4. Ezekiel 3:4 (NIV)

saturating every pore of their bodies, minds, and spirits. With rising exhilaration, they were utterly convinced that Jesus was at this very moment fulfilling his promise to send the Spirit to them, to dwell in them. In that moment, they understood many things that had been unclear before and felt they knew Jesus in a way they never had.

Inspired and directed by the Spirit, they spoke about the wonders of God as the Spirit gave them words—yet the words were in other languages. Matthew had just been thinking about how God spoke in different languages at Sinai, and now he himself was speaking in a language he had never learned. It was as if God were reversing the confusion of Babel, granting everyone the ability to understand each other perfectly, without obstacles.

The people flowed toward the southern exits, talking excitedly, wanting to tell everyone in the city about it, but also seeking to comprehend what was happening. They poured across the Temple courts, flooding the halls leading to the Southern Steps and the City of David.

The 120 were carried along with the crowd, conversing with the people around them. As they exited the Triple Gates, Peter stepped to one side, and in a great voice he thundered, "Fellow Jews, and all of you who live in Jerusalem!"

Startled, the surging crowd paused to see who was speaking. The people kept pouring out the gates and overflowed down the steps, completely filling the public areas all around them. Finally, they saw Peter at the top of the steps, his hand raised authoritatively.

Still buzzing, the crowd murmured to each other, wondering what it all meant. Some ventured sarcastically, "Maybe they began to drink a little early before they came today."

Unruffled, Peter spoke in a commanding voice, "Fellow Jews and all of you who live in Jerusalem, let me explain this to you; listen carefully to what I say. These men are not drunk, as you suppose. It's only nine in the morning. No, this is what was spoken by the prophet Joel:

"'*In the last days, God says, I will pour out my Spirit on all people.*

Your sons and daughters will prophesy, your young men will see visions, your old men will dream dreams. Even on my servants, both men and women, I will pour out my Spirit in those days, and they will prophesy. I will show wonders in the heaven above and signs on the earth below, blood and fire and billows of smoke. The sun will be turned to darkness and the moon to blood before the coming of the great and glorious day of the Lord. And everyone who calls on the name of the Lord will be saved.' [5]

"Men of Israel," Peter continued, "listen to this. Jesus of Nazareth was a man accredited by God to you by miracles, wonders, and signs, which God did among you through him, as you yourselves know. This man was handed over to you by God's set purpose and foreknowledge; and you, with the help of wicked men, put him to death by nailing him to the cross."

Caiaphas had been caught up in the crowd as it inexorably moved from the Temple courts to the Southern Steps. He tried to escape into the Chamber of Hewn Stone as they passed it, but the crowd was too strong. Now he was trapped among these common, naïve people. He scorned their simplicity. Yet, as Peter spoke persuasively, Caiaphas feared that many would believe Peter and desert Caiaphas. He ground his teeth as Peter's accusation about wicked men struck home. Now people around Caiaphas recognized him, and he saw their anger kindle against him.

Peter reclaimed their attention. "But God raised him from the dead! He freed him from the agony of death, because it was impossible for death to keep its hold on him. David said about him:

'I saw the Lord always before me. Because he is at my right hand, I will not be shaken. Therefore, my heart is glad and my tongue rejoices; my body also will live in hope, because you will not abandon me to the grave, nor will you let your Holy One see decay. You have made known to me the paths of life; you will fill me with joy in your presence.' [6]

---

5. Joel 2:28-32 (NIV)
6. Psalm 16:8-11 (NIV)

"Brothers, I can tell you confidently that the patriarch David died and was buried, and his tomb is here to this day."

The eyes of the crowd drifted to the west, where David's tomb shone in the morning sun.

"But he was a prophet and knew God had promised him on oath that he would place one of his descendants on his throne. Seeing what was ahead, he spoke of the resurrection of the Christ, that he was not abandoned to the grave, nor did his body see decay. God has raised this Jesus to life, and we are all witnesses of the fact."

Raising his voice further, Peter declared confidently, "Exalted to the right hand of God, Jesus has received from the Father the promised Holy Spirit and has poured out what you now see and hear. For David did not ascend to heaven, and yet he said,

'The Lord said to my Lord: "Sit at my right hand until I make your enemies a footstool for your feet.'[7]

"Therefore, let all Israel be assured of this: God has made this Jesus, whom you crucified, both Lord and Christ!"

When the people heard this, they were cut to the heart and said to Peter and the other apostles, "Brothers, what shall we do?"

Peter replied, "Repent and be baptized, every one of you, in the name of Jesus Christ for the forgiveness of your sins. And you will receive the gift of the Holy Spirit."

He paused briefly and studied their faces, connecting with their eyes and hearts, then said earnestly, "This promise is for you and your children and for all who are far off."

An expectant silence fell over the enormous multitude as Peter stopped speaking, sowing his invitation deep in their fertile hearts.

Forgiveness! The gift of the Holy Spirit! It seemed too incredible to be true. In one moment, they were condemned for rejecting and killing the Messiah, for whom they had waited for centuries. In the next, they were offered the chance to be forgiven and become followers of Jesus, now confirmed as the Christ!

---

7. Psalm 110:1 (NIV)

Peter's eyes swept over the crowd, praying for the Spirit to do his work of convicting the people of sin, righteousness, and judgment. The 120, scattered throughout the crowd, searched the faces of those next to them.

What would they decide?

Some of these people had been present in Galilee or Judea for Jesus' teaching and miracles. Some had celebrated with the throng coming down the Mount of Olives and onto the Temple Mount eight weeks before. Some had been part of the mob screaming for Jesus' crucifixion barely seven weeks earlier. Others had arrived at the Pentecost feast from other countries, hearing for the first time the incredible stories about the Galilean's ministry, powerful miracles, death, and resurrection.

What would they decide?

Would they learn from the Rabbi? Be forgiven by the sacrifice of the Lamb? Honor a new King? Become citizens of a new Kingdom? As if responding to an inaudible Voice, individuals stepped out of the crowds toward Peter, or drew near to one of the 120, whom they heard speaking in their languages.

Several young priests had heard Jesus in the Temple and were suddenly convinced. Old Nahshon, the Chief Shepherd from Bethlehem, had come to Jerusalem for the feast. The man who had loaned the donkey to Jesus for his triumphal entry to Jerusalem now offered his own life.

The families of Salmon and Ruth, and Jesse and Deborah, from Bethlehem, who had lost sons, would now become new sons and daughters of the King. Shlomo, a money changer, changed his heart. Rimon and his daughter Miryam, reconciled to each other, longed to be reconciled to God. A mother and son who had seen the ascension of Jesus in Bethany, had come up to the Temple that day with the father. All three now joined the others.

Procla, the wife of Pilate, was now convinced that the man in her dreams was truly from God. Even though she risked certain wrath and possible punishment from her husband, she stepped forward with a resolute confidence. And many more—young, old, men, women, rich, poor, Pharisees, Zealots, Samaritans, Herodians, powerful, powerless—all came to Jesus, the Son of Man and of God, confessing him as their new Lord.

Joyfully, Peter and the 120 split up and led the people in groups to the forty-eight different purification baths scattered around the plaza. Going down into the water one by one, they were baptized. Out of the water came the church redeemed by the Lamb, the King, the Prince of Peace, the Cornerstone—all combined in the person of Jesus, the Messiah.

That day about 3000 people believed and obeyed the good news about Jesus! When the baptisms were finished, everyone returned to the Temple courts to pray together and to praise God for their new family, planning to return each day to the Temple, to continue to learn about Jesus and life as citizens of the new Kingdom.

Reflect

1. Looking back over this book, what other people do you think Jesus might have visited, or what places he might have gone, or which ideas he would have planted?
2. What might Jesus say to you if he saw you after the tomb?

Learn

Jews present that day at Pentecost, as well as Jews today, would likely see strong connections between the first Pentecost when the Jews received the Law at Mount Sinai, and this Pentecost in the first century. Here are some striking connections:

- Sinai, first Pentecost/Jerusalem (Acts 2)
- 50 days after Exodus/50 days after cross
- Fire from God/Fire descends on disciples
- Thunder (*kol*, voice) with commandments/Peter preaches word from God about the and law Word (Jesus)
- Law is similar to marriage covenant/Church is the bride of Christ
- 3000 people die after making golden calf/3000 saved after baptism

Also, read these passages for more background information about Peter's sermon.

1. Readings at Pentecost in the Temple, Ex. 19:16-19, Ezek. 1:4-5, 12-13, 19-24; 3:4
2. 70 voices at Sinai, (https://www.sefaria.org/sheets/25573?lang=bi) Rabbi Yochanan said that in that way, the whole world could understand it. Also, Shemot Rabbah 5:9, a midrash (commentary) on the book of Exodus.
3. Numerous ideas in this section were also shared by Ray Vander Laan, mp3 12a, 12b, Shavuot, in his series of 30 lessons at Christ Memorial series, 1996. also mp3s 15A, 15B on Shavuot (Pentecost or Feast of Weeks)
4. Coming of the Holy Spirit, Acts 2:1-4
5. Speaking in other languages, Acts 2:4-12
6. Confusion of Babel, Gen. 11:7-9
7. Peter's speech, Acts 2:14-41
8. Pouring out Spirit on all people, Joel 2:28-32
9. David talking about Jesus, Ps. 16:8-11
10. The Lord said to my Lord, Ps. 110:1

Appendix A: Notes, Scriptures & References

Over 400 biblical references, plus other historical, cultural, geographical, or linguistic notes

Vignette 1: The Centurion Believes

1. Crucifixion, John 19:17-37
2. Jesus—It is finished. Jn. 19:30
3. Effects of Jesus' death. Matt. 27:51-53
4. References to Jerusalem in the time of Jesus.
    a. Bargil Pixner. With Jesus in Jerusalem.
    b. Leen Ritmeyer. Jerusalem in the time of Christ (power point). Ritmeyer archaeological design.

Vignette 2: Joseph of Arimathea and Pilate

5. Joseph asking for body, Matt. 27:57-61
6. Piercing Jesus' body Jn. 19:34
7. Trial before Pilate Jn. 18:33-38

Appendix A: Notes, Scriptures & References

Vignette 3: Caiaphas Celebrates

8. Trial with Caiaphas Matt. 26:57-68
9. Malchus Lu. 22:50ff
10. Jesus avoiding arrest, John 7:45-49; 8:59

Vignette 4: From the Cross to the Tomb

11. Burial Jn. 19:38ff, Mark 15:42-47
12. Psalm recited at the grave Ps. 116:3, 7, 15
13. Jesus gives Mary to John's care Jn. 19:26ff

Vignette 5: Peter's Dark Night

14. Peter's denial Lu. 22:31, 33, 54ff

Vignette 6: Anguish in Bethany

15. John calling down fire on a village Lu. 9:54
16. Jesus' words on cross, Ps. 22:1, 16, 18, 24

Vignette 7: Nicodemus' Confession

17. Sabbath Shema Deut. 6:4-9

Vignette 8: The Moment the World Changed Forever

18. Resurrection Mat. 27, Mr. 16, Lu. 24, Jn. 20
19. Reference to resurrection at Caesarea Philippi Mat. 16:21

Appendix A: Notes, Scriptures & References

Vignette 9: Jesus and Mary Magdalene

20. Jesus casting out demons from Mary Magdalene Mk. 16:9, Luke 8:2
21. Jesus appearing to Mary, John 20:11-18

Vignette 10: "He Does Not Treat Us as Our Sins Deserve"

22. Essene Gate, Ritmeyer, power point of Jerusalem in the time of Jesus, slides 28-29
23. Hinnom valley sacrifices 2 Chron. 33:6ff
24. Judas' betrayal, Matt. 26:47-50, 27:1-10
25. Judas hanging Mat. 27:5ff, Acts 1:15-19
26. Jesus forgiving Judas Lu. 23:34
27. Jesus' words while digging Ps. 103:8-12

Vignette 11: The Best Torah Lesson in History

28. Cleopas (variant Clopas) and Mary, Lu. 24:18, Jn. 19:25
29. Events of road to Emmaus Lu. 24:13ff
30. Points from Jesus' lesson from Moses and the prophets:
    a. Moses speaks about the prophet Dt. 18:15
    b. A virgin will conceive Is. 7:14
    c. The Messiah to be born in Bethlehem Mic. 5:2
    d. Shepherds of Bethlehem Lu. 2:8ff
    e. Slaughter in Bethlehem, Mt. 2:16ff, Jr. 31:15
    f. Jesus' family sent to Egypt Mt. 2:13-15
    g. Second Exodus from Egypt Mt. 2:23
    h. Hebrew word for Nazareth comes from *ntzer*, Branch Is. 11:1
    i. Suffering Servant Is. 42:1ff

APPENDIX A: NOTES, SCRIPTURES & REFERENCES

    j. Mend reeds and nourish flames Mt. 12:20
    k. All kinds of healing Lu. 4:18-19
    l. Blind, deaf, lame Is. 35:5-6
    m. Bread from heaven, Ex. 16, Mt. 14:14ff
    n. Living by physical and spiritual bread Mt. 4:4, Dt. 8:3
    o. Rock in the desert 1 Cor. 10:4, Ex. 17:1ff
    p. The Hebrew word, *mashiach*, and the Greek word *Christos*, both mean "Anointed One."
    q. King, gentle, riding on donkey Zc. 9:9, Mt. 21:5
    r. Shepherd fired by sheep, 30 pieces of silver, Zc. 11:12ff, Mt. 27:5
    s. Stone that causes people to stumble, Is. 8:14, Ps. 118:22-23
    t. Suffering Messiah Is. 53
    u. Passover Lamb whose blood protects people Ex. 12:21ff
    v. Scapegoat banished from the camp Lv. 16:20ff
    w. Look on bronze serpent to be saved Nu. 21:9
    x. Anguish on cross, forsaken by God Ps. 22
    y. Precious is the death of the saints Ps. 116:15
    z. Holy one wouldn't see decay, Ps. 16:10, Ac. 2:27
    aa. Near sacrifice of Isaac Gn. 22.
31. Jesus as symbolized in the feasts—Ray Vander Laan, material from class on the Passover

VIGNETTE 12: WHO ARE THESE PEOPLE? (PART 1)

32. Couple raised from the dead Matt. 27:53

VIGNETTE 13: CELEBRATION IN BETHANY

33. Lazarus brought to life John 11:31ff
34. Chief priests trying to kill Lazarus John 12:9-10

Appendix A: Notes, Scriptures & References

35. Jesus' visit to Mary and Martha the first time Lu. 10:38-42
36. David's quote Ps. 27:4-14

Vignette 14: The Intriguing Case of Lazarus

37. Jesus learning about Lazarus John 10:40, 11:4ff
38. Martha's reaction John 11:21ff
39. Eternal life John 17:3
40. Lazarus in heaven. Some concepts from Bodie and Brock Thoene, <u>When Jesus Wept</u> (Jerusalem Chronicles, book 1, pp. 263ff)
41. Elijah and Enoch 2 Kings 2:11, Gen. 5:24
42. Holy people raised from death and going to the city Matt. 27:53

Vignette 15: An Unforgettable Walk to Bethlehem

43. Pool of Siloam, John 9:7
44. Joseph and Mary in temple on 8th day Lu. 2:22ff
45. Mary treasuring things in her heart Lu. 2:19, 51, Matt. 6:19-21
46. Sarah, Abraham, Hagar, Ishmael, and Isaac. Gen. 16, 21
47. Woman caught in adultery Jn. 8

Vignette 16: Tragedy in Bethlehem, Revisited

48. Herod's purge of children Matt. 2:16ff
49. Magi's visit Matt. 2:1-12
50. Escape to Egypt, Matt. 2:13ff

Appendix A: Notes, Scriptures & References

Vignette 17: Jesus Confronts Caiaphas

51. Royal Stoa, Alec Garrard, The Splendor of the Temple, pp. 60-61
52. Chamber of Hewn Stone (Gazith), place of Sanhedrin, ibid.
53. Soldiers paid to spread rumor, Matt. 28:11-15
54. Witnesses to Jesus Jn. 5:31-47
55. Sham trial Matt. 26:59-67
56. Curtain torn Matt. 27:51, Heb. 10:19ff
57. Jerusalem hemmed in Lu. 19:41-44
58. Jesus as High Priest forever Heb. 7:23-28

Vignette 18: The "Man from the Dream" Visits Pilate and Procla

59. Pilate's wife Procla, https://en.wikipedia.org/wiki/Pontius_Pilate%27s_wife
60. Jesus before Pilate during trial Jn. 18:33-40, Matt. 27:11-26
61. Power over death Rom. 6:9-10
62. Barabbas released Lu. 23:25
63. Jesus is the Truth John 14:6

Vignette 19: Who are These People? (Part 2)

64. Rhoda, Mary, and the house Acts 12:12-13
65. Boy who hugged Jesus (Mark) Mar. 14:51
66. Saints raised from the dead Matt. 27:52-53
67. Various historical periods represented: Solomon and dedication of temple (I Ki. 8); Saul anointed (1 Sam. 10:24ff); Hezekiah's kingship (2 Chron. 32:1-5); exiles returned (Ezra 2:1ff); crossing the Jordan with Joshua

Appendix A: Notes, Scriptures & References

(Josh. 3); faithful remnant with Elijah (I Ki. 19:18); teenagers in the desert (Num. 14:29ff); Deborah's army (Judg. 4:14ff); land of Goshen (Gen. 4:5ff); servants of Abraham (Gen. 14:14-24).

68. Every promise "Yes" in Jesus 2 Cor. 1:20

Vignette 20: Return to Golgotha

69. Passover week. Pixner, with Jesus in Jerusalem, pp. 180-81.
70. Golgotha, Jn. 19:17-30
71. Scriptures at Golgotha, Ps. 30:3, 5
72. Piercing Mary's soul, Lu. 2:35
73. Longinus as centurion? https://en.wikipedia.org/wiki/Longinus
74. Jesus laying down and taking up his life John 10:17-18

Vignette 21: A New Vision for Bartimaeus

75. Spirit snatching Jesus up, Acts 8:39
76. Two Jerichos in the time of Jesus (Roman and ancient), https://apologeticspress.org/controversial-jericho-666/, https://www.britannica.com/place/Jericho-West-Bank
77. Is Jesus the Messiah? Matt. 11:2-6
78. Two blind men in Capernaum, Matt. 9:27-31.
79. Your faith has healed you. The Greek word *sozo* can mean both healed and saved; in fact, it is translated much more often "save" than "healed." (Strong's lexicon, word #4982).

Appendix A: Notes, Scriptures & References

Vignette 22: A Fresh Start for Zacchaeus

80. Four times over, Ex. 22:1
81. Jewish false shepherds; Jesus quoting, Ezek. 34:1-16
82. John preaching, Lu. 3:12ff

Vignette 23: Changed Woman, Changed Village

83. Sychar, the Samaritan woman, and the well Jn. 4
84. The man you are living with, Jn. 4:18
85. Temple on Mount Gerizim, Jn. 4:20; Ritmeyer, https://www.ritmeyer.com/2021/01/21/the-jerusalem-temple-on-mount-gerizim/
86. Tabernacle, Ex. 25-30
87. Temple, 1 Kings 5-8
88. In spirit and in truth, Jn. 4:24
89. Perfect sacrifice, Heb. 10:12
90. Spiritual temple, and every believer is a priest, 1 Pet. 2:4-9, Eph. 2:21-22
91. Man from Jerusalem, Acts 8

Vignette 24: The Grateful Leper

92. Pilgrimage paths from Galilee to Jerusalem, https://www.biblicalarchaeology.org/daily/biblical-topics/new-testament/3-pilgrimage-paths-from-galilee-to-jerusalem/
93. Border between Samaria and Galilee, Lu. 17:11ff; possibly the village of Burq'in today, about 1.5 miles west of Jenin today in northern Samaria, part of the West Bank. Map of Burq'in https://www.google.com/maps/dir/%D8%AC%D9%86%D9%8A%D9%86%E2%80%AD%E2%80%AD/%

Appendix A: Notes, Scriptures & References

D8%AC%D9%86%D9%8A%D9%86%E2%80%AD/@32.
42059,35.1812486,11z/data=
!4m14!4m13!1m5!1m1!1s0x151cfed5525459a7:
0x8af2eaf8c123e9a4!2m2!1d35.2938591!2d32.
4646353!1m5!1m1!1s0x151cfed5525459a7:
0x8af2eaf8c123e9a4!2m2!1d35.2938591!2d32.
4646353!3e0?hl=en

94. Nathan, Lu. 17:11-19 Nathan means "giver" in Hebrew.
95. Sebaste, name of the capital of Samaria under Herod the Great (formerly the city of Samaria)
96. Purity and impurity, Lev. 13
97. Overcome evil with good, Rom. 12:21
98. Protected from getting sick again. Mk. 9:25

Vignette 25: Two Trips to Heaven, Two Resurrections

99. Son of widow from Nain resurrected, Lu. 7:11-17
100. Daughter of Jairus resurrected, Luke 8:51-56
101. Cana, Jn. 2
102. Jairus' wife, Fulvia. A possible name mentioned in this article, https://www.stathanasius.org/site/assets/files/4500/study_11_06_16.pdf, from this footnote: Catherine van Dyke, tr., "The Letters of Pontius Pilate and Claudia Procula", Relics of Repentance, 1st Edition, Issana Press, Lincoln, NE 68503, 1990.
103. Angels carrying Rebecca, Lu. 16:22
104. Song of Miriam, Ex. 15
105. King Josiah, 2 Ki. 23:25

Vignette 26: Confessions at Breakfast

106. Fishing at night and the catch, John 21

Appendix A: Notes, Scriptures & References

107. Second miraculous catch—the first in Luke 5:1-11
108. Soldiers letting the apostles go at the arrest, John 18:8.
109. Mark's garment, Mark 14:51-52.
110. Jesus and Peter's restoration. John 21:15ff

Vignette 27: Day of Testimony

111. Synagogue service in Jesus' time, https://www.jstor.org/stable/3140264?seq=4#metadata_info_tab_contents.
112. Passages read by Jesus at synagogue, Ps. 146:7-9, Is. 35:5-10.
113. Signs in Capernaum greater than those in foreign cities, Matt. 12:41-42, Lu. 11:20-24.
114. Testimonies of Jesus' ministry—boy with loaves and fishes, Jn. 6:8; woman with flow of blood Lu. 8:43ff; Roman centurion and servant, Lu. 7:1-10; two blind men, Mat. 9:27ff; demon-possessed and mute man, Matt. 9:32ff; paralytic, Lu. 5:15ff.
115. Law requirement of two or three witnesses establish something: 91 bible verses mention this! See this link: https://www.openbible.info/topics/two_or_three_witnesses
116. Kingdom of God suffering violence, Matt. 11:12
117. Kingdom is the narrow way, Matt. 7:14.
118. Weighing the cost, Lu. 14:28-33
119. Kingdom costs everything, Matt. 13:44-46

Vignette 28: Supper at Matthew's House

120. Supper at Matthew's house, Matt. 9:10-13.
121. Coin that smells like fish, Matt. 17:27
122. Jael, Lu. 15:2
123. Rahab, Josh. 2, 6

Appendix A: Notes, Scriptures & References

124. First banquet in heaven, Matt. 8:11ff
125. "Put away", Deut. 24:1, Matt. 1:19
126. Meal out of nothing, Matt. 14:13ff, Matt. 15:29ff
127. Peacemakers and daughters of God, Matt. 5:9
128. Selling possessions to help, Acts 2:45, 4:34-35, Prov. 19:17, Matt. 6:4
129. Engraved on hearts, 2 Cor. 3:3
130. Stories never written, John 21:25

Vignette 29: A New Celebration

131. Peter's mother-in-law, Lu. 4:38ff, Matt. 8:14ff

The word "rebuke" (Greek *epitimao*) is used in Lu. 4:39 (fever), 4:41 demons), and Matt. 8:26 (storm) to accomplish God's will. Five times in Matthew 8, Jesus accomplishes God's will with a word.

132. Shema, Deut. 6:4-5
133. Creation and new shalom, Gen. 1
134. Bread in Jesus' hands...Matthew 14, 15
135. I will not drink this fruit again... Matt. 26:29

Vignette 30: A Sober Delivery from Joseph of Arimathea

136. Using anything for good Rom. 8:28
137. The Messiah took our sins and suffering on him, Isaiah 53:4-12
138. What Caiaphas meant for evil... Gen. 50:20
139. Jesus dying in spite of sin...Rom. 5:8
140. Those who have been given a trust must prove faithful 1 Cor. 4:2

Appendix A: Notes, Scriptures & References

Vignette 31: Taming the Sons of Thunder

141. Peter finds Jesus, Mark 1:36
142. Crowds and disciples sent away, Matt. 14:22ff
143. Our bodies like Jesus 1 John 3:2, Phil. 3:21. Credit to Randy Alcorn, *Heaven*, for expanding this idea.
144. John not dying, John 21:21-23
145. Faraway places, Ephesus and I, 2, 3 John
146. Unexpected places, Rev. 1
147. Wondrous sites and small tastes, Matt. 17:1ff
148. Sons of Thunder, Mark 3:17
149. James and John called to follow, Matt. 4:21
150. Seeking special honor, Mar. 10:35
151. Serving or being served, Mark 10:45
152. Washing feet, John 13
153. Fire from heaven, Lu. 9:52-55, 1 Kings 18:37-38
154. Jairus' daughter, Lu. 8:53ff
155. Transfiguration, Matt. 17
156. Praying in the Garden, Matt. 26:37
157. Father who began this work... Philippians 1:6

Vignette 32: Life in Cana After the Wedding

158. Reprisals of Romans against Jews in Galilee, https://en.wikipedia.org/wiki/Siege_of_Yodfat
159. Enemies, Matt. 5:44-46
160. The miracle in Cana, Jn. 2:1-11
161. Significance of water to wine, Doug Ponder, https://tabletalkmagazine.com/posts/why-did-jesus-turn-water-into-wine/

Appendix A: Notes, Scriptures & References

Vignette 33: Reckoning Time for Antipas

162. Which Herod is this? Herod Antipas, https://en.wikipedia.org/wiki/Herod_Antipas, https://www.catholicweekly.com.au/which-herod-was-which-sorting-out-the-five-herods/4/
163. History of Sepphoris, https://www.land-of-the-bible.com/Sepphoris_The_Forgotten_City
164. Chuza, Herod's steward, Luke 8:1-3
165. First visit of Antipas and Jesus, Lu. 23:8-12
166. Slaughter of babies, Matt. 2:16ff
167. Herod arresting and killing John the Baptist Mark 6:17-29
168. Lived in luxury, James 5:1-6
169. What Antipas should have done—based on Isaiah 58:6-14.
170. Times of refreshing, Acts 3:19
171. Choose life, Deut. 30:19

Vignette 34: A Second Chance to Follow

172. Rich young ruler, Mark 10:17-22
173. Pearl, Matt. 13:45-46
174. Father caring for you, Matt. 6:31-33
175. Bury my father, Matt. 8:21
176. Other excuses, Lu. 14:18ff
177. Hate family, Lu. 14:25-33
178. Samaritan village refusing Jesus, Lu. 9:52ff
179. Eye for an eye, Ex. 21:24
180. Treating strangers as Jesus, Matt. 25:40ff
181. Counting the cost, Lu. 14:25ff

Appendix A: Notes, Scriptures & References

Vignette 35: The Delivered Decapolis Demoniac

182. Decapolis city of Susita, https://www.youtube.com/watch?v=3Ey7cV5p_vE
183. Kursi, https://www.biblewalks.com/kursi
184. Casting out demons from the Gergesene demoniac, Matt. 8:28-34, Mark 5:1-20, Lu. 8:26-39.
185. Abishua means "my father is rescue (safety), or "my father is opulence"
186. Jesus being cast out, John 1:11
187. Feeding of the four thousand, Matt. 15:29ff
188. City set on a hill, Matt. 5:14

Vignette 36: The Circle Closes—Coming Near to God Again

189. First reading, Gen. 3:22-24
190. Second reading, Ex. 33:7-11
191. Third reading, Ex. 40:34-39
192. Fourth reading, 1 Kings 8:6-11
193. Rebuilding of temple and Jerusalem, Ezra and Nehemiah
194. Creator to created, John 1:10ff
195. You have seen God, John 14:9ff
196. How to live in the Kingdom of heaven, Matt. 5-7, 13, other passages
197. High Priest forever, Heb. 7:16-17, 21-22
198. Changing priesthood, changing law, Heb. 7:12
199. Perfect sacrifice once for all, Heb. 7:27-28, 9:11-14, 23-26
200. All foods clean, Mark 7:19
201. Ways of worship, Ps. 66, 95, 149, 150
202. Promise of Jeremiah, Jer. 31:33-34
203. Emmanuel, Matt. 1:23, God came near

Appendix A: Notes, Scriptures & References

Vignette 37: Lunch with the Rabbi of Nazareth

204. Tree of life, Ps. 1
205. Exodus story, Passover, Ex. 11-12
206. Jesus in Jerusalem, age 12, Lu. 2:41-52.
207. Obedient in suffering, Heb. 5:8-9, Phil. 2:8
208. Nazareth synagogue service, Lu. 4:16ff
209. *Ntzer* is the Hebrew word for "branch" (Is. 11:11), one of the terms for the Messiah, on whom the Spirit of the Lord would rest. The name of the town of Nazareth comes from this word, reflecting their belief that the Messiah would come from their village. So instead of Jesus being called a Nazarene because he came from there, the town of Nazareth was named for the expected Messiah; it was named for Jesus!
210. Some who always doubted, Mark 6:5-6
211. Veil over their eyes, or not, 2 Cor. 3:14-16, Lu. 7:8-10.

Vignette 38: Storytime Under the Olive Tree

212. I am the way, John 14:2-6
213. God caring for us in heaven, Rev. 21:1-7
214. The city of God, Rev. 21:9-27
215. Sharing everything, Acts. 4:32-35
216. If this were not so, I would have told you… John 14:2-6

Vignette 39: Would You Like to Write a Gospel?

217. The three major divisions of the Jewish Old Testament were the Torah (Law), the Navim (Prophets), and the Ketuvim (Writings). The Jews combined the first letter of each of these sections and formed the word Tanakh,

Appendix A: Notes, Scriptures & References

which is their word for the Old Testament. In fact, for many Jews who do not believe in Jesus as the Messiah, they do not accept the New Testament as their Bible. So they don't have the Old and New Testaments, but rather just the Tanakh. Also, some of the books in the Hebrew Tanakh are combined differently than our Old Testament. For example, 1-2 Samuel are one book, as are 1-2 Kings and 1-2 Chronicles. What we call the 12 Minor Prophets are one book in the Tanakh. This type of change results in a total of 24 books in the Hebrew Tanakh, not 39 books as many accept it. For more information about the Hebrew Bible, see https://en.wikipedia.org/wiki/Hebrew_Bible#:~:text=In%20Tiberian%20Masoretic%20codices%2C%20including,%2C%20Esther%2C%20Daniel%2C%20Ezra.

218. David's words, Ps. 25:4, 5, 14
219. Holy Spirit's role in writing, John 14:26, 15:26, 16:13-15
220. Good news...from the Greek word for gospel, *euaggelio*
221. Too many stories, John 21:25

Vignette 40: Get out of the Boat!

222. Peace, be still, Mk. 4:39
223. Psalms...89:9, 107:29-30.
224. Walking on the water, Job 9:8
225. All things are possible with God, Mark 10:27
226. Fix your eyes on Jesus, Heb. 12:2
227. Dry land, Ex. 14:21, Josh. 3:17
228. They would do the things Jesus did, John 14:12
229. Preaching, healing, casting out demons, Matt. 10:1,8; Luke 10:17

Appendix A: Notes, Scriptures & References

Vignette 41: A Special Wedding in Caesarea Philippi

230. Paulus and Lucas, Mark 9:14ff
231. Alara, Matt. 15:21ff
232. In the image of God, Gen. 1:27, 5:1
233. Gates of Hades at Caesarea Philippi, Matt. 16:13-20

Vignette 42: More than 500—the Galilean Believers

234. Appeared to 500 at the same time, 1 Cor 15:4-8
235. Malachi's prophecy, Mal. 4:2
236. Zechariah's prophecy, Lu. 1:76-79
237. Wise and foolish men, Matt. 7:24-27
238. Vine, following, John 15:1-25
239. Rejoice in persecution, Matt. 5:10-12
240. Accuser's actions, John 8:44, 10:10
241. Trumpet call, Matt. 24:31, 1 Cor. 15:51-52
242. Kingdom and inheritance, Matt. 25:34
243. I told you ahead of time, Matt. 24:25
244. Be perfect, Matt. 5:48
245. The Father will carry on his work in you, Phil. 1:6

Vignette 43: I Give You My Mind and Spirit

246. Many wished to see what you see, Matt. 13:17, 1 Pet. 1:10-12
247. Sovereign Lord, Is. 40:10
248. Tends the flock, Is. 40:11
249. I am the good shepherd, John 10:11
250. Cannot snatch them out of my hand, John 10:28

Appendix A: Notes, Scriptures & References

251. Who can fathom the Spirit, Is. 40:13
252. No eyes, ears, minds...Is. 64:4, 1 Cor. 2:9
253. Only the Spirit knows, 1 Cor. 2:10-12
254. Spirit will make known... John 16:15
255. Jesus is head of the church, Eph. 5:23
256. You are the body of Christ, 1 Cor. 12:27

Vignette 44: You Will Drink the Cup I Drink

257. Two ways, Matt. 7:13-14
258. Conversation on Mount of Olives, Matt. 24:4-51
259. Caesarea Philippi, Jesus' weapons, Matt. 16:21-27
260. Cup, baptism, giving lives, Mark 10:39, 45
261. Words of Jesus about suffering, Matt. 10:5-42
262. Give you words, Matt. 10:19
263. Spirit to teach and remind, John 14:26
264. Authority, Matt. 28:18-20, 16:19, Luke 10:19
265. Power to do many things, Matt. 10:8-9, Mark 16:17-18
266. Spiritual weapons for a spiritual war, Eph. 6:10-16
267. Do what my Father shows you, John 5:19
268. Take you into glory, Ps. 73:24
269. For sources about the apostles' possible deaths, see these links and many other sites:

- https://amazingbibletimeline.com/blog/q6_apostles_die/
- https://www.gotquestions.org/apostles-die.html
- https://overviewbible.com/how-did-the-apostles-die/

Vignette 45: The Testimony of the Risen Saints

270. Abraham and Mount Moriah, Gen. 22
271. The rescue of Lot, Gen. 14
272. Melchizedek and Abraham, Gen. 14:17ff

Appendix A: Notes, Scriptures & References

273. God did not spare his son, Rom. 8:32
274. He is our peace, Eph. 2:14
275. Bread and wine, Matt. 26:26ff
276. Moses sending out spies, Num. 13
277. Manna and quail, Ex. 16
278. Water from the rock, Ex. 17, Num. 20
279. The word in Hebrew for desert (or literally, "place of speaking") in Hebrew is *midbar*. The three main consonants of the root are d, b(or soft v), and r. Other words that use that root are *debir* (Most Holy Place), *Dober* (pasture), *davar* (word or speak), and *deber* (plague or pestilence). Strong's concordance (words #4057, 1696-99). It is possible that as the Jews saw this root, they would recall all these meanings, and connect the meanings, perhaps in this way: "The desert (*midbar*) is the Holy Place (*debir*) where God takes his sheep to pasture (*dober*), to speak to them (*davar*)." And they also suffered plagues in the desert! This concept was mentioned also by Ray Vander Laan.
280. Jesus is true bread from heaven, John 6:32, 41, 50, 51
281. Jesus as living Stone, who is also bread, 1 Pet. 2:4, Matt. 4:3
282. Jesus is living water, John 4:14, 7:37
283. Robes of righteousness, Is. 61:10
284. Jesus as shepherd, John 10, 1 Pet. 5:4
285. 70 years in exile, Jer. 25:10, 29:10
286. Rebuilding of altar and temple, Ezra 3.
287. Great menoroth in Court of Prayer, Mishnah in Sukkkot 5:2-3, Garrard p. 66, https://www.sefaria.org/Mishnah_Sukkah.5.6?lang=bi
288. Jesus inviting people to come to him and drink, John 7:37
289. Jesus the light of the world, John 8:12ff
290. Many put their faith in him. John 8:30
291. Final blessing, Num. 6:24-26

Appendix A: Notes, Scriptures & References

Vignette 46: We Were Blind, but Now We See

292. Blind man and pool of Siloam, John 9

Vignette 47: He Stopped Sinning, and Something Better Happened to Him

293. Crippled man at Bethesda, John 5
294. Something worse, John 5:14

Vignette 48: New Life After Being Rescued

295. Woman caught in adultery, John 7:53-8:11

Vignette 49: Final words, Final Miracle

296. Ascension, Luke 24:50-52, Acts 1:6-11
297. Priestly blessing, Num. 6:23-26
298. Angel's comments, Acts 1:11

Vignette 50: Pentecost in the Temple: the Church is Born

299. The word for purification baths in Hebrew is *Mikva'oth*. They are like baptisteries, which were used by the Jews to fully submerge themselves in order to be pure before worshipping God in places like the Temple or synagogue.
300. Readings at Pentecost in the Temple, Ex. 19:16-19, Ezek. 1:4-5, 12-13, 19-24; 3:4
301. 70 voices at Sinai, https://www.sefaria.org/sheets/25573?lang=bi Rabbi Yochanan said that in that way the whole

Appendix A: Notes, Scriptures & References

world could understand it. Also, Shemot Rabbah 5:9, a midrash (commentary) on the book of Exodus.

302. Numerous ideas in this section about the similarities and contrasts between the first Pentecost at Mount Sinai, and this Pentecost in Acts 2, were also shared by Ray Vander Laan, mp3 12a, 12b, Shavuot, in his series of 30 lessons at Christ Memorial series, 1996. Similarities of Acts 2 to Sinai, Ex. 19-20, 32. Also see 2 Corinthians 3:7-18.
303. Coming of the Holy Spirit, Acts 2:1-4
304. Speaking in other languages, Acts 2:4-12
305. Confusion of Babel, Gen. 11:7-9
306. Peter's speech, Acts 2:14-41
307. Pouring out Spirit on all people, Joel 2:28-32
308. David talking about Jesus, Ps. 16:8-11
309. The Lord said to my Lord, Ps. 110:1

Appendix B: Resources Consulted

Books

- Alcorn, Randy. *Heaven*. Carol Stream, Ill: Tyndale House Publishing, 2011.
- Bahat, Dan. The Carta Jerusalem Atlas. Jerusalem: CARTA Jerusalem, 2011.
- Bateman IV, Herbert W., Bock, Darell L., and Johnston, Gordan H. *Jesus the Messiah: Tracing The Promises, Expectations, And Coming of Israel's King*. Grand Rapids: Kregel Academic, 2012.
- Bishop, Jim. *The Day Christ Died*, Harper and Brothers: 1957, pp. 219-224.
- Bolen, Todd. Pictorial Library of Bible Lands. https://www.bibleplaces.com/pictorial-library-of-bible-lands/
- Bolen, Todd. Photo Companion to the Bible. https://www.bibleplaces.com/photo-companion-to-the-bible/
- Garrard, Alec. *Splendor of the Temple*. Grand Rapids: Kregel Publications, 2000.

Appendix B: Resources Consulted

- Isbouts, Jean-Pierre. *In the footsteps of Jesus: A Chronicle of his Life and the Origins of Christianity*. Washington: National Geographic Society, 2012
- Logos Bible software, Faithlife publishing, www.logos.com.
- May, Herbert G., editor, in consultation with Hunt, G.N.S and Hamilton, R.W. Oxford Bible Atlas, (2nd ed.) London: Oxford University Press, 1974.
- Pixner, Bargil. *With Jesus in Jerusalem: his first and last days in Judea*. Rosh Pina: Corazin Publishing, 2005.
- Pixner, Bargil. *With Jesus through Galilee, according to the fifth Gospel*. Rosh Pina: Corazin Publishing, 1992.
- Ritmeyer, Leen, "Jerusalem in the time of Christ" (PowerPoint), Ritmeyer archaeological design.
- Ritmeyer, Leen and Kathleen, *Jerusalem in the year 30 AD*. Carol Stream, Ill: Tyndale House Publishers, 2015.
- Strong, James. Enhanced Strong's lexicon, in Logos library.
- Strong, James. *Strong's Exhaustive Concordance of the Bible*. Henderson: Henderson Academic Publishing, 2009.
- Thoene, Brock and Bodie, *When Jesus Wept*. (Jerusalem Chronicles, book 1) Grand Rapids: Zondervan Publishing, 2013.
- Vander Laan, Ray. Cassette series at Christ Memorial church, Holland, MI.

Appendix B: Resources Consulted

Internet sites

Apostles' Deaths

- https://amazingbibletimeline.com/blog/q6_apostles_die/
- https://www.gotquestions.org/apostles-die.html
- https://overviewbible.com/how-did-the-apostles-die/
- https://amazingbibletimeline.com/blog/q6_apostles_die/
- https://www.gotquestions.org/apostles-die.html
- https://overviewbible.com/how-did-the-apostles-die/

Ascension

- https://en.wikipedia.org/wiki/Ascension_of_Jesus#cite_note-FOOTNOTEMcDonald200422-25
- https://dannythedigger.com/ascension/

Burial Customs and Spices

- http://www.bibleresearch.org/observancebook5/b5w79.html

Casting Lots

- https://bibletruthpublishers.com/casting-lots/ljm21467
- https://en.wikipedia.org/wiki/Cleromancy

Decapolis

- https://www.jw.org/en/library/books/Insight-on-the-Scriptures/Decapolis/

Appendix B: Resources Consulted

Disciples on the Road to Emmaus

- The Unnamed Emmaus disciple: Mary, wife of Cleopas? Jones, Victoria Emily. https://artandtheology.org/2017/04/28/the-unnamed-emmaus-disciple-mary-wife-of-cleopas/

- Who were the disciples on the road to Emmaus? Boice, James. https://www.christianity.com/jesus/death-and-resurrection/resurrection/who-were-the-disciples-on-the-road-to-emmaus.html; https://en.wikipedia.org/wiki/Road_to_Emmaus_appearance

Distances on Roads Used in the First Century

- http://www.ctlibrary.com/ch/1998/issue59/59h028.htmlCentury

Eleona Grotto

- https://aleteia.org/2019/01/26/the-three-mystical-grottoes-of-the-holy-land/

Essenes

- https://en.wikipedia.org/wiki/Essenes
- https://www.wm.edu/offices/auxiliary/osher/course-info/classnotes/whitedeadseascrollsthefirstfollowers.pdf
- https://bibleinterp.arizona.edu/articles/mcnamer

Events at the Tomb on Resurrection Sunday

- https://answersingenesis.org/jesus/resurrection/christs-resurrection-four-accounts-one-reality/

Appendix B: Resources Consulted

Events of Jesus' Ministry

- https://interactivelifeofjesus.com/a-complete-list-of-events-in-the-life-of-jesus/
- https://www.biblewalks.com/jesusfootsteps

Family of Jesus

- https://en.wikipedia.org/wiki/History_of_Joseph_the_Carpenter
- https://www.baslibrary.org/biblical-archaeology-review/28/6/13

Fulvia, Jairus' Wife

- A possible name mentioned in this article: https://www.stathanasius.org/site/assets/files/4500/study_11_06_16.pdf, from this footnote: Catherine van Dyke, tr., "The Letters of Pontius Pilate and Claudia Procula", Relics of Repentance, 1st Edition, Issana Press, Lincoln, NE 68503, 1990.

Herod: Which Herod is This? Herod Antipas

- https://en.wikipedia.org/wiki/Herod_Antipas, https://www.catholicweekly.com.au/which-herod-was-which-sorting-out-the-five-herods/4/

James, the Half-brother of Jesus

- https://www.newworldencyclopedia.org/entry/James_the_Just
- https://www.wm.edu/offices/auxiliary/osher/course-info/classnotes/whitedeadseascrollsthefirstfollowers.pdf

- https://en.wikipedia.org/wiki/Gospel_of_the_Hebrews, Jerome, De viris illustribus 2

Jerichos in the Time of Jesus (Roman and Ancient)

- https://apologeticspress.org/controversial-jericho-666/, https://www.britannica.com/place/Jericho-West-Bank

Jesus in the Old Testament

- https://www.gordonconwell.edu/blog/jesus-in-the-old-testament/
- https://www.wordsoffaithhopelove.com/jesus-in-the-old-testament-types/
- https://en.wikipedia.org/wiki/Old_Testament_messianic_prophecies_quoted_in_tthe_New_Testament
- https://www.jesusfilm.org/blog-and-stories/old-testament-prophecies.html

Joseph of Arimathea

- https://www.researchgate.net/publication/347096428_What_You_May_Not_Know_About_Joseph_of_Arimathea
- https://d.lib.rochester.edu/camelot/text/history-of-that-holy-disciple-joseph-of-arimathea#:~:text=But%20now%2C%20though%20Joseph%20of,in%20private%3A%20insomuch%20that%20he

Kenites

- https://www.jewishencyclopedia.com/articles/9279-kenites

Appendix B: Resources Consulted

Keys to the Kingdom

- https://en.wikipedia.org/wiki/Power_of_the_Keys; https://torahportions.ffoz.org/disciples/matthew/keys-to-heaven.html; https://www.jerusalemperspective.com/2766/

Kursi

- https://www.biblewalks.com/kursi

Law Requirement of Two or Three Witnesses

- https://www.openbible.info/topics/two_or_three_witnesses

Longinus as Centurion

- https://en.wikipedia.org/wiki/Longinus

Menoroth in Court of Prayer

- Mishnah in Sukkot 5:2-3, Garrard p. 66,
- https://www.sefaria.org/Mishnah_Sukkah.5.6?lang=bi

Maps

- https://www.biblewalks.com/jesusfootsteps
- https://www.biblewalks.com/jesus_maps

Miracles of Jesus' Ministry

- https://www.christianity.com/jesus/life-of-jesus/miracles/what-miracles-did-jesus-perform.html

Omer

- https://en.wikipedia.org/wiki/Counting_of_the_Omer
- https://www.hebrew4christians.com/Holidays/Spring_Holidays/Sefirat_HaOmer/sefirat_haomer.html

Pentecost (Shavuot)

- https://www.myjewishlearning.com/article/shavuot-history-from-the-bible-to-Temple-times/

People in Gospels

- https://en.wikipedia.org/wiki/Category:People_in_the_canonical_gospels

Philip the Tetrarch

- https://en.wikipedia.org/wiki/Philip_the_Tetrarch

Places Jesus Visited

- http://www.about-jesus.org/jesus-places-map.htm

Procla, Pilate's Wife

- https://en.wikipedia.org/wiki/Pontius_Pilate%27s_wife

Remez

- https://www.thattheworldmayknow.com/remez)

Appendix B: Resources Consulted

Reprisals of Romans Aagainst Jews in Galilee

- https://en.wikipedia.org/wiki/Siege_of_Yodfat

Ritmeyer Archaeological Design

- www.ritmeyer.com.

Sepphoris

- https://www.land-of-the-bible.com/Sepphoris_The_Forgotten_City

Susita

- https://www.youtube.com/watch?v=3Ey7cV5p_vE

Synagogue Service in Jesus' Time

- https://www.jstor.org/stable/3140264?seq=4#metadata_info_tab_contents.

Tanakh Jewish Old Testament

- https://en.wikipedia.org/wiki/Hebrew_Bible#:~:text=In%20Tiberian%20Masoretic%20codices%2C%20including,%2C%20Esther%2C%20Daniel%2C%20Ezra.

Temple on Mount Gerizim

- Jn. 4:20
- Ritmeyer, https://www.ritmeyer.com/2021/01/21/the-jerusalem-Temple-on-mount-gerizim/

APPENDIX B: RESOURCES CONSULTED

Vander Laan. About Education in Jesus' Time

- https://www.thattheworldmayknow.com/rabbi-and-talmidim

Water to Wine, Doug Ponder

- https://tabletalkmagazine.com/posts/why-did-jesus-turn-water-into-wine/

Appendix C: Maps & Images

This section includes the following maps and pictures:

- Topographical map of Israel—3D View to the Northeast
- Political Borders at the Time of Jesus (Sons of Herod and Procurators)
- Jesus' Public Galilean Ministry
- Jesus in Jerusalem
- Plain of Gennesaret, from Southwest (with labels)
- Second Temple Model: Jerusalem in Jesus' Time

Topographical map of Israel—3D View to the Northeast

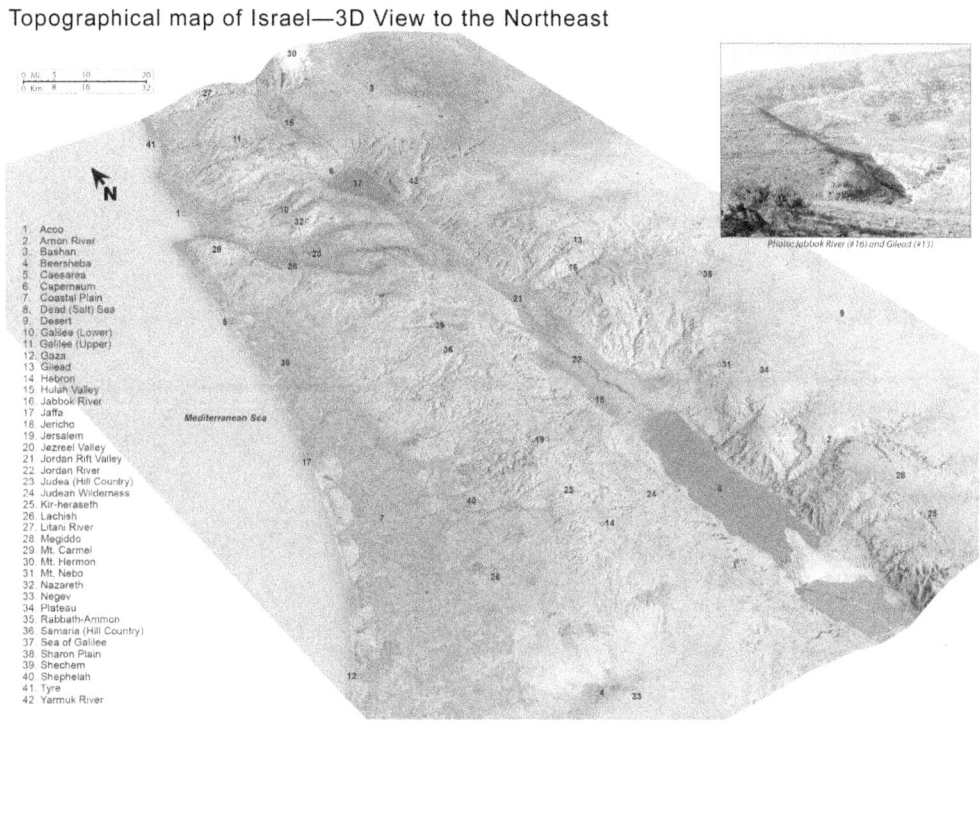

1. Acco
2. Arnon River
3. Bashan
4. Beersheba
5. Caesarea
6. Capernaum
7. Coastal Plain
8. Dead (Salt) Sea
9. Desert
10. Galilee (Lower)
11. Galilee (Upper)
12. Gaza
13. Gilead
14. Hebron
15. Hulah Valley
16. Jabbok River
17. Jaffa
18. Jericho
19. Jerusalem
20. Jezreel Valley
21. Jordan Rift Valley
22. Jordan River
23. Judea (Hill Country)
24. Judean Wilderness
25. Kir-heraseth
26. Lachish
27. Litani River
28. Megiddo
29. Mt. Carmel
30. Mt. Hermon
31. Mt. Nebo
32. Nazareth
33. Negev
34. Plateau
35. Rabbath-Ammon
36. Samaria (Hill Country)
37. Sea of Galilee
38. Sharon Plain
39. Shechem
40. Shephelah
41. Tyre
42. Yarmuk River

Photo: Jabbok River (#16) and Gilead (#13)

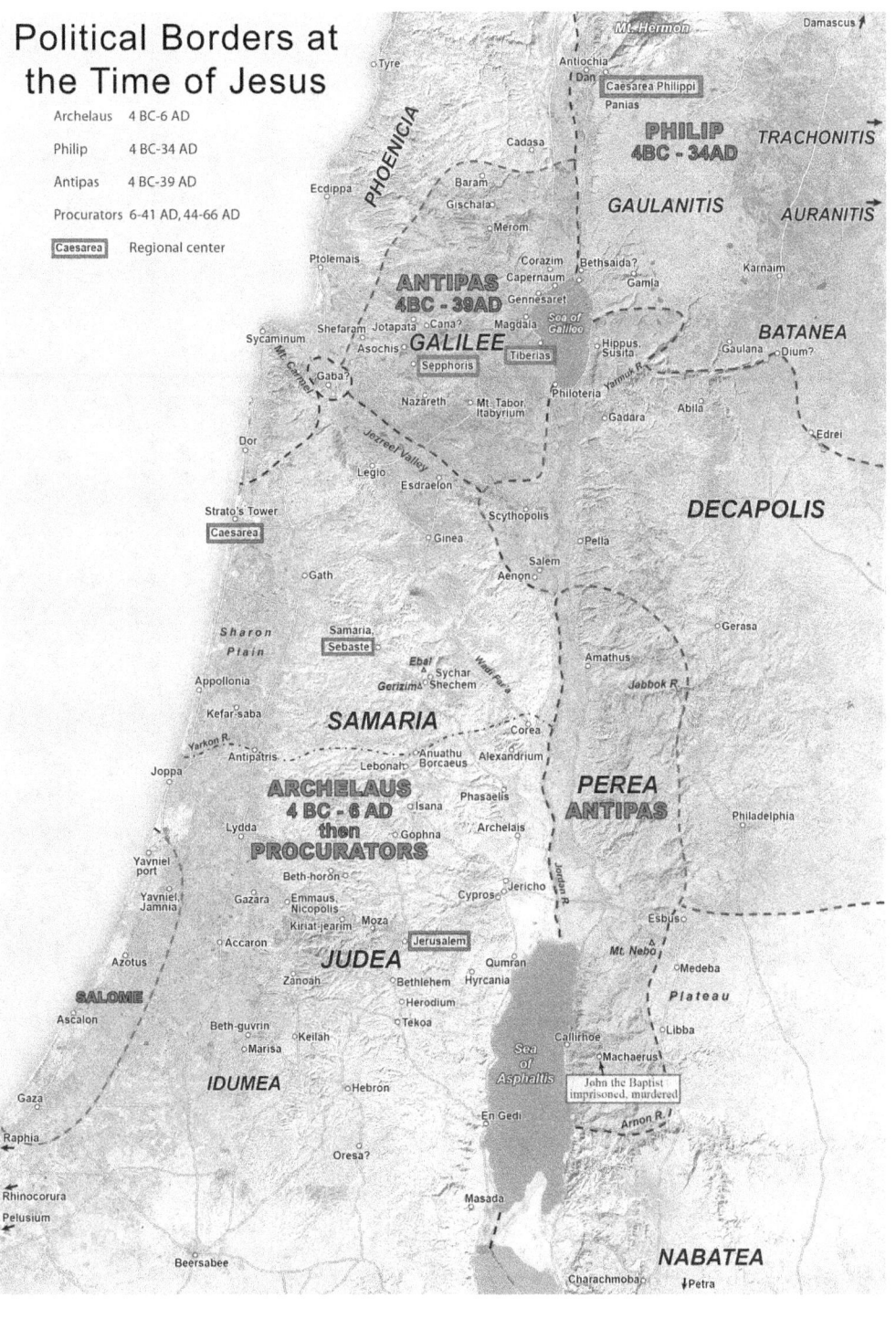

Jesus' Public Galilean Ministry

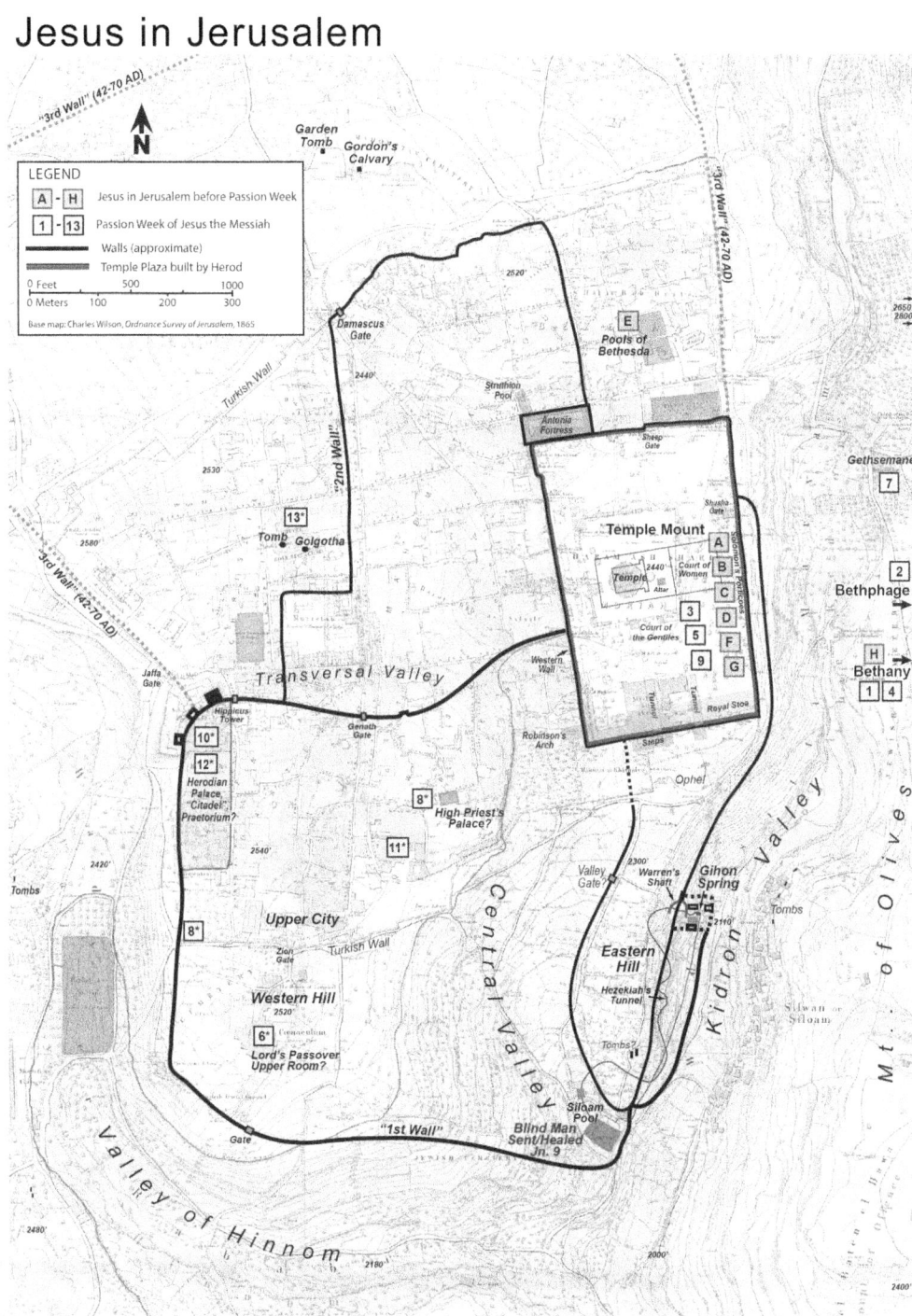

Second Temple Model: Jerusalem in Jesus' Time

Acknowledgments

I'm grateful to the Lord for giving me the idea for this book and the experiences, knowledge, and qualities that helped me complete it. I also thank so many who have helped me expand my knowledge in biblical text, geography, history, and culture: John Walker (first took me to Israel); Nedal Juneidi (our guide in Israel); Ray Vander Laan (Jewish backgrounds); Todd Bolen (photography of Bible lands); Leen Ritmeyer (archaeology of Jerusalem and the Temple Mount); and many authors of inspirational Biblical literature/fiction, such as Max Lucado, Bodie Thoene, Francine Rivers, and Randy Alcorn.

About the Author

Stephen Austin is from Abilene, Texas. He earned bachelors, masters, and doctoral degrees in biblical studies and ministry from Abilene Christian University. He and his wife and family served the church in Buenos Aires, Argentina for 7 years and then an inner-city church in Houston for 7 years. He has served as the founding director of the Texas International Bible Institute full-time since 2005. He has edited a hymnal of praise and worship music and classic hymns, in Spanish, *Cantos del Camino*, which has been distributed to every US state and every country in Latin America. He has traveled widely in Latin America to give seminars and conferences, to encourage and train churches and leaders. He and his wife Lynette love spending time with their married children and one wonderful grandchild, as well as traveling with friends to different countries. He also enjoys teaching, reading, singing, racquet sports, and golf.

You May Also Like:

Biblical Fiction from Scrivenings Press:

***A Certain Man* by Linda Dindzans**
***A Certain Future*—Book One**

Mara is a young Samaritan beginning to discover her love for Samuel—and his for her. Soon she will be deemed mature enough to marry. Her hopes are dashed when her greedy father brokers a match with the cruel son of the wealthy High Priest of Shechem. When her loathsome betrothed is killed, her beloved Samuel must run for his life. Mara and Samuel struggle to survive and reunite during the treacherous and scandalous times of the Bible under the merciless rule of Rome.

Along the way, they are entangled within the snares of such notable figures as King Herod, Herodias, Pontius Pilate, Caiaphas, and Salome.

The heartrending tales of Mara and Samuel are interwoven with their desperate love story. Before either meets Yeshua the Nazarene face to face.

Before He sets the political, religious, and spiritual landscape on fire. And before either Mara or Samuel are immortalized in the gospels.

Get your copy here:

https://scrivenings.link/acertainman

New Star by Lana Christian

Book One of The Magi's Encounters

How far would you go to protect what you believe in?

Akilah, a highly respected priest-scholar in Magi society, considers all his astronomy discoveries well-deserved stepping-stones to a more fulfilling life. But the appearance of a new star challenges his priorities. As Persia totters on the brink of an undesirable king coming to power, Akilah declines a position that could turn that tide. Instead, he studies a star that doesn't appear in any almanac or religious writings. Except Jewish.

When he and his colleagues uncover a few Jewish prophecies linking the star to an eternal king, Akilah becomes the target of Persia's religious and governmental conflicts. Jailed for crimes he didn't commit, Akilah must rely on questionable resources to free himself and reach Jerusalem.

Persia's purists aren't the only ones bent on keeping their country free of Jewish influences. As dangers at home and abroad plunge Akilah and his colleagues into three countries' religious conflicts and circumstances beyond their imagining, Akilah realizes his knowledge of Jesus could potentially destroy Magi society and its power over Persia's official religion and government. Untrusting of his Council, a thousand miles from aid, and bound in a potentially career-ending contract, Akilah must decide how far he will go to protect what he knows of Jesus—and whether the cost of his belief is worth the risk.

Get your copy here:

https://scrivenings.link/newstar

Stay up-to-date on your favorite books and authors with our free e-newsletters.

ScriveningsPress.com

www.ingramcontent.com/pod-product-compliance
Lightning Source LLC
Chambersburg PA
CBHW052132070526
44585CB00017B/1790